PUBLISHER'S NOTE

V&S Publishers has carved a significant niche in the publishing industry over the last decade, having successfully published more than 1000 titles across 9 languages spanning over 50 subject categories. Being known for the quality of content, we have built a reputation of excellence and reliability. We have consistently delivered **"Value & Substance"** to our readers, through a wide range of titles across a variety of genres covering school books, fiction and non-fiction that caters to different people from every section of the society.

The **Olympiad Guidebooks for classes 1-10** across all subjects, launched almost a decade ago, under the **GEN X Imprint**, became a go-to-source for the school students in no time, owing to their invaluable and substantive content written in a guidebook pattern,.

Having successfully sold a million copies of the same and in response to demand by both students as well as shopkeepers nationwide; we now present before you our newly launched **Olympiad Workbook Series**, designed for **classes 1-10 across 4 subjects**.

The workbooks are meticulously curated by a team of experienced educators, researchers and subject matter experts, edited by professionals and peer reviewed by teachers. The team has poured its efforts and expertise into creating a crisp and concise workbook which will help and guide the students to the path of success in Olympiad exams. The **MCQs** identified will not only help in scoring top marks in Olympiads but also inculcate a sense of deeper understanding of the subject, by way of solving **HOTS** and referring to complete solutions at the end of the book.

Here we present our new release– **OLYMPIAD WORKBOOK (NCO) CLASS-7** having following features:

- Based on the latest syllabi
- MCQs with comprehensive coverage of topics
- HOTS Questions liberally included
- A dedicated chapter on logical reasoning
- Model test paper for thorough practice
- Sample OMR sheet for real time simulation

We have made sure through our best efforts, that this workbook strictly follows the latest syllabi and patterns of the Olympiad Examination.

As **V&S Publishers** continuously strive to enhance the readability and maintain the credibility of our academic publications, we seek the support of our valuable readers in influencing and enriching the lives of future generations of students.

P.S. While every care has been taken to ensure the correctness of the content, if you come across any error, howsoever minor, do not hesitate to discuss with teachers while pointing that out to us in no uncertain terms.

We wish you all the best for your exams!

DISTINCTIVE FEATURES

OLYMPIAD WORKBOOK

Published by:

V&S PUBLISHERS

F-2/16, Ansari road, Daryaganj, New Delhi-110002
☎ 23240026, 23240027 • *Fax:* 011-23240028
✉ info@vspublishers.com • 🌐 www.vspublishers.com

 **Online Brandstore: amazon.in/vspublishers**

Regional Office : Hyderabad
5-1-707/1, Brij Bhawan (Beside Central Bank of India Lane)
Bank Street, Koti, Hyderabad - 500 095
☎ 040-24737290
✉ vspublishershyd@gmail.com

Follow us on:   

BUY OUR BOOKS FROM: AMAZON FLIPKART

© **Copyright:** *V&S* PUBLISHERS
ISBN 978-81-978176-5-6
New Edition

DISCLAIMER

CONTENTS

CONTENTS

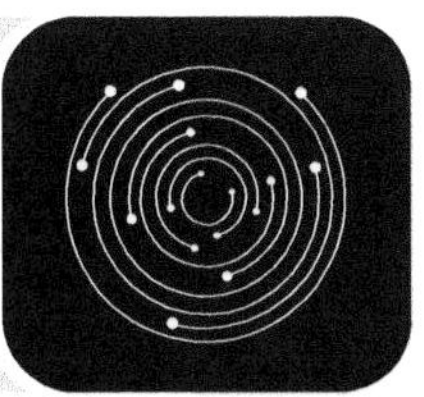

FUNDAMENTALS OF COMPUTER

LEARNING OBJECTIVES

- ➤ Hardware components
- ➤ Output devices
- ➤ Using Internet Explorer
- ➤ Input Devices
- ➤ Software concepts
- ➤ Using Windows

MULTIPLE CHOICE QUESTIONS

1. Which of the following is an example of mobile computers?
   - (A) Laptop
   - (B) Desktop computers
   - (C) Cray-1
   - (D) SDS 92

2. Which is the supercomputer developed in India?
   - (A) Param
   - (B) Anurag
   - (C) Abacus
   - (D) Both (a) and (b)

3. What is the given strips of black lines called?

   - (A) Strip code
   - (B) Bar code
   - (C) Line code
   - (D) Bill code

4. What device is used for reading cheques in India?
   - (A) Scanner
   - (B) OMR
   - (C) Bar code reader
   - (D) MICR

5. Find the correct statement(s).
   - (i) Supercomputers are used for weather forecasting.
   - (ii) Supercomputers are used for rocketing and plasma physics.
   - (iii) Processing speed of microcomputer lies in the range of 10-30 MIPS.
   - (iv) Mainframe computers are less powerful than the mini computers.
   - (A) Only I & II are correct
   - (B) I, II & III are correct
   - (C) III & IV are correct
   - (D) All are correct

6. Which device is used to scan the input and convert it into a computer file?
   - (A) Key board
   - (B) Mouse
   - (C) Scanner
   - (D) Microphone

7. Which is the device used for checking a multiple answer sheet?
   - (A) OMR
   - (B) OCR
   - (C) MICR
   - (D) Light pen

8. What is meant by double click?
   - (A) Pressing the left button of the mouse.
   - (B) Holding the left button and moving.

(C) Pressing the right button of the mouse twice.

(D) Quickly clicking left mouse button twice.

9. Web camera is a/an ______ device.

(A) Input

(B) Output

(C) Memory

(D) Both (a) and (b)

10. OCR stands for ______.

(A) Optical Card Reader

(B) Optical Calculator Reader

(C) Optical Card Reader

(D) Optical Character Recognition

11. Which card contains a magnetic strip and can store information magnetically?

(A) Smart card

(B) PAN card

(C) Credit card

(D) Grocery cards

12. Which is specially used for printing graphs, maps, and charts?

(A) Printer

(B) Plotter

(C) Modem

(D) Speaker

13. Which device is used for transferring files to other computers (of the network) without any damage?

(A) Speaker

(B) Mouse

(C) Plotter

(D) Modem

14. What is the result displayed on the monitor called?

(A) Soft copy

(B) Hard copy

(C) Duplicate copy

(D) Inkjet printer

15. Which printer gives output in Braille text?

(A) Impact printer

(B) Laser printer

(C) Braille printer

(D) Inkjet printer

16. Modem is a/an ______ device.

(A) Input

(B) Output

(C) Recording

(D) Both (a) and (b)

17. Microphone accepts ______ as input.

(A) Sound

(B) Pictures

(C) typed data

(D) video

18. Which type of plotters use jets of ink instead of ink pens?

(A) A flatbed plotter

(B) An inkjet plotter

(C) A micrographic plotter

(D) A ddrum plotter

19. Which kind of software performs the maintenance work of computer?

(A) Packages

(B) Utility software

(C) Computers

(D) Assembler

20. Which of these was an operating system?

(A) MS DOS

(B) MS Paint

(C) MS Office

(D) MS Front page

21. Given below is an image of an area marked by A that allows you to jump to parent folders or subfolder in the path of the current folder. What is the name of this Window?

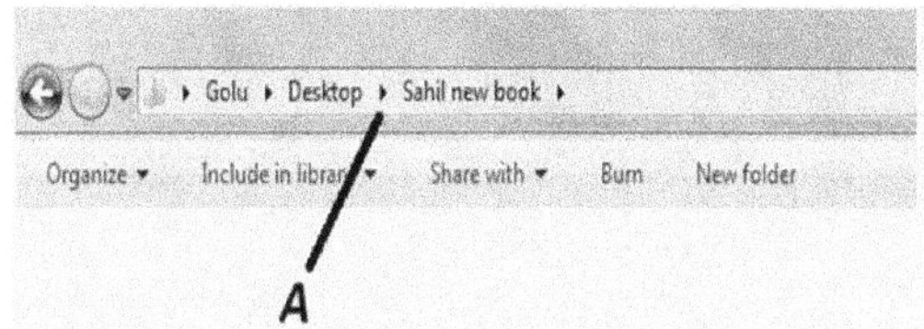

    (A) Breadcrumb
    (B) Jump trail
    (C) Navigation trail
    (D) Bread jump trail

22. Which of the following is not a difference between blu-ray disc and DVD?
    (A) The production cost of DVD is more than that of Blu-ray disc.
    (B) Read only memory type is not available in blu-ray whereas DVD supports read only memory.
    (C) Blu-ray disc uses violet-blue laser, where as DVD uses red laser.
    (D) A single layer blu-ray disc can store up to 25 GB data whereas a single layer DVD can store only 4, 7 GB of data.

23. What is the correct formula to calculate the transfer rate of a disk?
    (A) Data transfer in one revolution × rotational speed of disk.
    (B) No. of sectors per track × No. of bytes per track.
    (C) No. of sectors per track × rotational speed of disk.
    (D) No. of bytes per track × rotational speed of disk.

24. Which type of plotters uses jets of ink instead of ink pens?
    (A) A flatbed plotter
    (B) An inkjet plotter
    (C) A micro graphic plotter
    (D) A drum plotter

25. Arrange the following in ascending order of ease of access:
    1. Primary memory
    2. Secondary memory
    3. Cache memory
    (A) 3,2,1   (B) 2,1,3
    (C) 1,2,3   (D) 3,1,2

Darken Your Choice with HB Pencil

1.	Ⓐ Ⓑ Ⓒ Ⓓ	6.	Ⓐ Ⓑ Ⓒ Ⓓ	11.	Ⓐ Ⓑ Ⓒ Ⓓ	16.	Ⓐ Ⓑ Ⓒ Ⓓ	21.	Ⓐ Ⓑ Ⓒ Ⓓ
2.	Ⓐ Ⓑ Ⓒ Ⓓ	7.	Ⓐ Ⓑ Ⓒ Ⓓ	12.	Ⓐ Ⓑ Ⓒ Ⓓ	17.	Ⓐ Ⓑ Ⓒ Ⓓ	22.	Ⓐ Ⓑ Ⓒ Ⓓ
3.	Ⓐ Ⓑ Ⓒ Ⓓ	8.	Ⓐ Ⓑ Ⓒ Ⓓ	13.	Ⓐ Ⓑ Ⓒ Ⓓ	18.	Ⓐ Ⓑ Ⓒ Ⓓ	23.	Ⓐ Ⓑ Ⓒ Ⓓ
4.	Ⓐ Ⓑ Ⓒ Ⓓ	9.	Ⓐ Ⓑ Ⓒ Ⓓ	14.	Ⓐ Ⓑ Ⓒ Ⓓ	19.	Ⓐ Ⓑ Ⓒ Ⓓ	24.	Ⓐ Ⓑ Ⓒ Ⓓ
5.	Ⓐ Ⓑ Ⓒ Ⓓ	10.	Ⓐ Ⓑ Ⓒ Ⓓ	15.	Ⓐ Ⓑ Ⓒ Ⓓ	20.	Ⓐ Ⓑ Ⓒ Ⓓ	25.	Ⓐ Ⓑ Ⓒ Ⓓ

MEMORY AND STORAGE DEVICES

LEARNING OBJECTIVES

➤ Different memory and storage devices
➤ Types of computer memory and their usage

MULTIPLE CHOICE QUESTIONS

1. Digits used to represent characters in computer's memory are collectively called as _______.
   (A) Bits
   (B) Pits
   (C) Pixels
   (D) Dpi

2. Which of the following data storage device includes flash memory with a USB interface?
   (A) Jump drive
   (B) Optical disc drive
   (C) Magnetic disk drive
   (D) Floppy disk drive

3. A _________ can hold up to 25 times more data than a CD-ROM.
   (A) CD-R
   (B) CD-RW
   (C) DVD-ROM
   (D) Both (A) and (B)

4. _________ is a data storage device user integrated circuit assemblies as memory to store data persistently.
   (A) CD-ROM
   (B) Tape drive

   (C) SSD
   (D) DVD

5. A memory card _________.
   (A) Has a fixed storage capacity
   (B) Is small circular plastic card
   (C) Is a volatile storage medium
   (D) All of these

6. You are not able to work with images on your computer. You are also not able to run several programs easily on your computer. Your computer keeps giving messages like "Insufficient Memory for this Operation".

   Upgrading which of the following components may solve the above problem?
   (A) RAM
   (B) Processor
   (C) CD drive
   (D) Sound card

7. In which of the following storage devices the access time varies according to the storage location?
   (A) Random access storage device
   (B) Sequential access storage device

(C) Primary access storage device

(D) Secondary access storage device

8. Identify the following:

It is typically integrated directly within the CPU chip.

It improves processing by acting as a temporary high speed holding area between the main memory and CPU.

(A) RAM

(B) CD

(C) ROM

(D) Cache Memory

9. Which of the following statements is INCORRECT about EPROM?

(A) EPROM stands for Erasable Programmable Read Only Memory.

(B) It is volatile in nature.

(C) It comes in several sizes and storage capacities.

(D) Its data can be erased and new data can also be added to it.

10. What is the significance of dual layer optical disc over single layer disc?

(A) It stores significantly more data.

(B) It is smaller in size.

(C) It provides data compression.

(D) It is possible to write data in dual layer disc whereas in single layer disc, it was not.

11. When evaluating magnetic tapes, which of the following statements does not hold true?

(A) Data on a tape is accessed and processed sequentially.

(B) It is a secondary storage device.

(C) It is the fastest medium for storing and accessing data.

(D) The surface can record data by magnetization.

12. Which of the following is not a secondary storage medium on a computer?

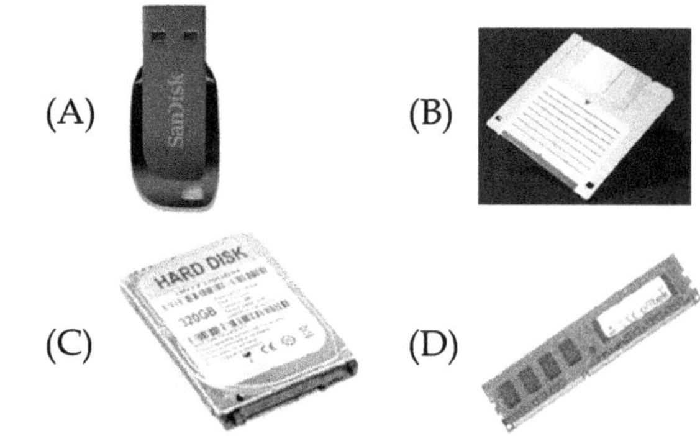

(A)   (B)   (C)   (D)

13. Complete the give diagram by replacing the X, Y and Z with the following Option.

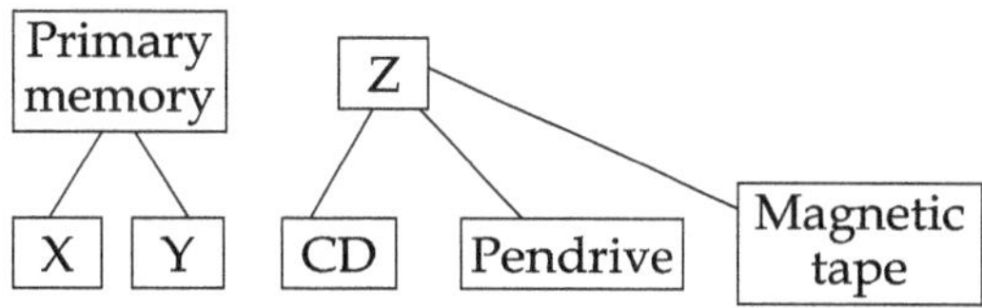

(A) X - RAM; Y - ROM; Z - Auxiliary memory

(B) X - RAM; Y - ROM; Z - Secondary memory

(C) X - Hard disk; Y - RAM; Z - Secondary memory

(D) Both (A) and (B)

14. Match the following.

Column-I	Column-II
(i) RAM	(a)
(ii) Hard disk drive	(b)
(iii) Floppy	(c)

(A) (i) - (b), (ii) - (c), (iii) - (a)

(B) (i)- (c), (ii) - (a), (iii) - (b)

(C) (i)- (a), (ii) - (c), (iii) - (b)

(D) (i)- (a), (ii) - (b), (iii) - (c)

15. Which of the following cannot be used for mass storage of digital data?
   (A) Hard disk drive
   (B) RAM
   (C) Optical disc drive
   (D) Optical jukebox

16. Identify the following:
   i.   It is used as main memory in personal computers.
   ii.   Inside its chip, each memory holds one bit of information.
   iii. It is made up of two parts, a transistor and a capacitor.
   (A) Dynamic RAM
   (B) Static RAM
   (C) Video RAM
   (D) Audio RAM

17. Which of the following statements is INCORRECT about an SD card?
   (A) You can lock/unlock the write operation using the write protection notch.
   (B) A direction notch on the card indicates which side should be inserted first in the electronic equipment.
   (C) It is temporary or volatile memory.
   (D) The label of the memory card contains vendor identification.

18. Which of the following is NOT a difference between Blu-ray disc and DVD?
   (A) The quality of audio and video recorded on Blu-ray disc is higher than DVDs.
   (B) Read only memory type is not available in Blu-ray disc whereas DVD supports read only memory,
   (C) Blu-ray disc uses violet-blue laser, whereas DVD uses red laser.
   (D) A single layer blu-ray disc can store upto 25 GB data whereas a single layer DVD can store only 4.7 GB of data.

19. What is the difference between Volatile and Non-Volatile Memory?
   (A) They are both same types of memory.
   (B) Volatile loses its contents when there is no electricity while non-volatile retains its content with or without electricity.
   (C) Non-volatile loses its contents when there is no electricity while volatile retains its content with or without electricity.
   (D) None of these

20. What is the role of an actuator in a hard-disk drive?
   (A) It moves the read-write arm.
   (B) It magnetize the platter.
   (C) It rotates the platter at high speed.
   (D) It controls the flow of data to and from the platter.

21. The other name for secondary memory is
    (A) Storing memory
    (B) Saving memory
    (C) Backup memory
    (D) None of these

22. The common type of memory module that consists of either 30 or 72 pins.
    (A) Single In-Line Memory Module (SIMM)
    (B) RAM (Random Access Memory)
    (C) ROM (Read Only Memory)
    (D) All of the above

23. What is the primary function of the BIOS (Basic Input/Output System) chip?
    (A) To create a backup of data
    (B) To control input and output operations
    (C) To initialize hardware components and start the boot process
    (D) To provide additional processing power to the CPU

24. Which storage device has the highest storage capacity among the options listed?
    (A) Hard Drive
    (B) Optical Drive
    (C) Solid-State Drive (SSD)
    (D) USB Flash Drive

25. What type of memory is used to store the computer's firmware and BIOS?
    (A) RAM
    (B) ROM
    (C) Cache
    (D) Register

—Darken Your Choice with HB Pencil—

1. Ⓐ Ⓑ Ⓒ Ⓓ	6. Ⓐ Ⓑ Ⓒ Ⓓ	11. Ⓐ Ⓑ Ⓒ Ⓓ	16. Ⓐ Ⓑ Ⓒ Ⓓ	21. Ⓐ Ⓑ Ⓒ Ⓓ
2. Ⓐ Ⓑ Ⓒ Ⓓ	7. Ⓐ Ⓑ Ⓒ Ⓓ	12. Ⓐ Ⓑ Ⓒ Ⓓ	17. Ⓐ Ⓑ Ⓒ Ⓓ	22. Ⓐ Ⓑ Ⓒ Ⓓ
3. Ⓐ Ⓑ Ⓒ Ⓓ	8. Ⓐ Ⓑ Ⓒ Ⓓ	13. Ⓐ Ⓑ Ⓒ Ⓓ	18. Ⓐ Ⓑ Ⓒ Ⓓ	23. Ⓐ Ⓑ Ⓒ Ⓓ
4. Ⓐ Ⓑ Ⓒ Ⓓ	9. Ⓐ Ⓑ Ⓒ Ⓓ	14. Ⓐ Ⓑ Ⓒ Ⓓ	19. Ⓐ Ⓑ Ⓒ Ⓓ	24. Ⓐ Ⓑ Ⓒ Ⓓ
5. Ⓐ Ⓑ Ⓒ Ⓓ	10. Ⓐ Ⓑ Ⓒ Ⓓ	15. Ⓐ Ⓑ Ⓒ Ⓓ	20. Ⓐ Ⓑ Ⓒ Ⓓ	25. Ⓐ Ⓑ Ⓒ Ⓓ

EVOLUTION OF COMPUTER

➤ History of Computers
➤ Different generations of computer

MULTIPLE CHOICE QUESTIONS

1. 4th and 5th generation of computers are powered by ______ chip.
   (A) Mercury
   (B) Silicon
   (C) Thermal
   (D) Wafer

2. First generation computers were
   (A) Efficiently marketed to spread them for use in various businesses
   (B) Computers used for mainly scientific calculations
   (C) Having speeds in microseconds (millionth/sec)
   (D) Running on sophisticated software

3. Which of following is not a feature of second generation computers?
   (A) Transistors were used
   (B) Core memory was developed
   (C) Programming in mechanical language
   (D) Easier to program than first generation computer

4. Data and information is temporarily stored in _________.
   (A) Central processing unit
   (B) Motherboard
   (C) Data bus
   (D) RAM

5. Which of these is not a major data processing function of a computer?
   (A) Gathering data
   (B) Processing data into information
   (C) Analyzing data or information
   (D) Storing the data or information

6. __________ operating system helped to put Microsoft on the computing map of world.
   (A) Unix   (B) Basic
   (C) DOS   (D) Fortan

7. _________ is the first name of two co-founder of Apple.Inc.
   (A) Bill   (B) Steve
   (C) Paul   (D) Heraldo

8. This computer language is made up of 0's and 1's and it is the basic computer code.
   (A) Fortan   (B) Pascal
   (C) Basic   (D) Binary

9. When representing letters, numbers and special characters in a binary language, we use combination of _________.
   (A) Eight bytes
   (B) Eight characters
   (C) Eight nibbles
   (D) Eight bits

10. The technologies used in commonly used PCs and the Apple Macintosh are based on different __________.
   (A) Platforms
   (B) Applications
   (C) Frames
   (D) Storage devices

11. Small, efficient, and economical PC-based servers have replaced __________ in several businesses.
   (A) Micro computers
   (B) Clients
   (C) Laptops
   (D) Mainframe

12. A marvel of technology, the __________ are the computers that perform complex scientific calculations.
   (A) Servers
   (B) Supercomputers
   (C) Laptops
   (D) PDA

13. Which of following is not a first generation computer?
   (A) ENIAC
   (B) UNIVAC-1
   (C) EDVAC
   (D) CDC

14. It was launched in 1950s. It was known to be the first commercially produced computer.
   (A) Zues Z3
   (B) UNIVAC-1
   (C) ENIAC
   (D) Harvard Mark I

15. It was used at the U.S Census Bureau in 1950. It was the first stored program computer in US that was successfully installed at a distant site after being moved from its site of manufacture.
   (A) UNIVAC-1101
   (B) Sinclair VX80
   (C) EDVAC
   (D) PDP 11

16. UNIVAC was used in 1952 to predict the outcome of a US presidential election. The election was contested between __________.
   (A) Franklin D. versus Thomas H.
   (B) Dwight D Eisenhower versus Adlai Stevenson
   (C) Harry Truman versus Thomas H.
   (D) All of these

17. Which of the following computer game was created by Steve Russell, Martin Graetz and Wayne Wiitanen?
   (A) Galaga
   (B) SpaceWar
   (C) Pong
   (D) Paperboy

18. The BASIC programming language was developed in 1964 by two professors of this college of __________.
   (A) Stanford
   (B) California
   (C) Dartmouth
   (D) Oxford

19. First ARPANET email is known to be sent in __________.
   (A) 1965
   (B) 1971
   (C) 1982
   (D) 1991

20. It is science. It tries to produce machines like computers and robots. They display intelligence similar to human beings. This is __________.
   (A) Biotechnology
   (B) Cross-over technology
   (C) Simulation
   (D) Artificial Intelligence

21. ______ is a kind of mass storage device. It is used for archiving read-only data that needs on-line access, but where access time is not very critical.

 (A) Disk Array

 (B) Automated Tape Library

 (C) CD-ROM Jukebox

 (D) None of these

22. Select the incorrect match.

 (A) Word's fastest super computer-Tianhe-2 (TH-2)

 (B) Example of Hard disk-Floppy disk

 (C) None-book-MacBook

 (D) Search Engine-Lycos

23. ________ a 16-bit minicomputer, was the first polish minicomputer, created at Elwro by a team led by scientist Jacek Karpinski.

 (A) MTTS 8800

 (B) K-202

 (C) PDP-8

 (D) PDP-11

24. Match the following.

 (i) Memory Address Register — (a) Holds address of next instruction to be executed.

 (ii) Memory Buffer Register — (b) Holds address of active memory location.

 (iii) Program Control — (c) Holds an instruction while it is being executed.

 (iv) Instruction — (d) Holds information on its way to end from memory.

 (A) (i)-(a), (ii)-(b), (iii)-(c), (iv)-(d)
 (B) (i)-(a), (ii)-(c), (iii)-(d), (iv)-(b)
 (C) (i)-(b), (ii)-(d), (iii)-(a), (iv)-(c)
 (D) (i)-(b), (ii)-(d), (iii)-(c), (iv)-(a)

25. Identify it.
 A. It is flash memory card.
 B. It is developed by Toshiba.
 C. It has contact pins that connect directly on the surface of the card.

 (A) Compact flash
 (B) SmartMedia Card
 (C) Secure Digital Card
 (D) Memory Stick

WINDOWS 10

LEARNING OBJECTIVES

➤ Basic concepts of Windows 10
➤ Working on windows
➤ Shortcuts of Windows

MULTIPLE CHOICE QUESTIONS

1. Microsoft Windows is a-
   (A) Word Processing Program
   (B) Database Program
   (C) Operating System
   (D) Graphics Program

2. What is the 'Start' menu in a standard personal computer?
   (A) Hardware part
   (B) An option and set of commands
   (C) Nothing, only status bar
   (D) Network related

3. What is Windows Explorer?
   (A) Personal Computer
   (B) Network
   (C) File Manager
   (D) Drive
   (E) Web Browser

4. All the deleted files go to
   (A) Recycle Bin
   (B) Task Bar
   (C) Tool Bar
   (D) Computer

5. Date and time are available on the desktop at
   (A) Keyboard
   (B) Recycle Bin
   (C) My Computer
   (D) Task Bar

6. Menus are the part of
   (A) hardware
   (B) user interface
   (C) status bar
   (D) monitor
   (E) None of these

7. Windows 10 released in
   (A) 2015
   (B) 2008
   (C) 2009
   (D) 2010

8. Which of the following shortcut keys is used to close current or active window?
   (A) Alt + F4
   (B) Ctrl + F4
   (C) Alt + F6
   (D) Ctrl + F6
   (E) Ctrl + Esc

9. A/An _________ contains programs that can be selected.
   (A) pointer
   (B) menu
   (C) icon
   (D) button

10. The desktop of a computer refers to
    (A) the visible screen
    (B) the area around the monitor
    (C) the top of the mouse pad
    (D) the inside of a folder

11. Factor making Windows popular is
    (A) multitasking capacity
    (B) desktop features
    (C) user friendly
    (D) being inexpensive

12. What are .bas, .doc, .htm examples of in computing?
    (A) Extensions
    (B) Protocols
    (C) Database
    (D) Domains

13. The extension of paint file is/are
    (A) .png
    (B) .jpg
    (C) .bmp
    (D) All of these

14. The steps involved to open a document are
    (A) select the document to open from the File down menu
    (B) click on the Open option in the Tools menu
    (C) Both 1 and 2
    (D) can be different for different Word document
    (E) None of the above

15. _________ lets you leave a screen or program.
    (A) Boot
    (B) Programs
    (C) Exit
    (D) Text

16. Which of the following keys is used to delete characters to the left of the cursor?
    (A) Alt + Delete
    (B) Shift
    (C) Esc
    (D) Delete
    (E) Backspace

17. _________ menu type is also known as a drop down menu.
    (A) Fly-down
    (B) Pop-down
    (C) Pop-up
    (D) Pull-up
    (E) Pull-down

18. To shrink a window to an icon,
    (A) open a group window
    (B) minimize a window
    (C) maximize a window
    (D) restore a window

19. A symbol or question on the screen that prompts you to take action and tell the computer what to do next, is
    (A) scanner
    (B) questionnaire
    (C) information seeker
    (D) prompt and dialog box
    (E) None of these

20. What is the default file extension for all Word documents?
    (A) WRD
    (B) TXT
    (C) DOC
    (D) FIL
    (E) WD

21. Which of the following shortcut keys represents the correct sequence for copy, paste and cut commands?
    (A) Ctrl + V; Ctrl + C; Ctrl + V
    (B) Ctrl + C; Ctrl + V; Ctrl + X
    (C) Ctrl + X; Ctrl + C; Ctrl + V
    (D) Ctrl + C; Ctrl + X; Ctrl + V

22. Why do you log-off from your computer when going out from your office?
    (A) Someone might steal your files, passwords, etc
    (B) In order to save electricity
    (C) Logging off is essential to increase performance
    (D) Logging off is mandatory before you go out
    (E) Logging off is a good exercise to perform regularly

23. What menu is selected to cut, copy and paste?
    (A) File
    (B) Tools
    (C) Special
    (D) Edit

24. A clipboard
    (A) is used to save data on disk in the event of a power failure
    (B) is able to retain the contents even when computer is switched OFF
    (C) is available only in Microsoft Word
    (D) is a temporary storage in computer memory and temporarily stores the cut or copied data
    (E) None of the above

25. A computer message is "Do you really want to delete the selected file (s)"? The user clicks 'Yes' key. It is called
    (A) program response
    (B) user output
    (C) user response
    (D) program output

Darken Your Choice with HB Pencil

	A B C D		A B C D		A B C D		A B C D		A B C D
1.	Ⓐ Ⓑ Ⓒ Ⓓ	6.	Ⓐ Ⓑ Ⓒ Ⓓ	11.	Ⓐ Ⓑ Ⓒ Ⓓ	16.	Ⓐ Ⓑ Ⓒ Ⓓ	21.	Ⓐ Ⓑ Ⓒ Ⓓ
2.	Ⓐ Ⓑ Ⓒ Ⓓ	7.	Ⓐ Ⓑ Ⓒ Ⓓ	12.	Ⓐ Ⓑ Ⓒ Ⓓ	17.	Ⓐ Ⓑ Ⓒ Ⓓ	22.	Ⓐ Ⓑ Ⓒ Ⓓ
3.	Ⓐ Ⓑ Ⓒ Ⓓ	8.	Ⓐ Ⓑ Ⓒ Ⓓ	13.	Ⓐ Ⓑ Ⓒ Ⓓ	18.	Ⓐ Ⓑ Ⓒ Ⓓ	23.	Ⓐ Ⓑ Ⓒ Ⓓ
4.	Ⓐ Ⓑ Ⓒ Ⓓ	9.	Ⓐ Ⓑ Ⓒ Ⓓ	14.	Ⓐ Ⓑ Ⓒ Ⓓ	19.	Ⓐ Ⓑ Ⓒ Ⓓ	24.	Ⓐ Ⓑ Ⓒ Ⓓ
5.	Ⓐ Ⓑ Ⓒ Ⓓ	10.	Ⓐ Ⓑ Ⓒ Ⓓ	15.	Ⓐ Ⓑ Ⓒ Ⓓ	20.	Ⓐ Ⓑ Ⓒ Ⓓ	25.	Ⓐ Ⓑ Ⓒ Ⓓ

MS WORD 

5

➤ Basics of MS Word
➤ Working in MS Word
➤ Mail Merge

MULTIPLE CHOICE QUESTIONS

1. Split cell __________.
   (A) Splits all the cells of the table in to two equal halves
   (B) Requires the number of columns or rows to be created in the cell to be split
   (C) Requires the number of columns and rows and redraws a table
   (D) Combines two or more cell

2. The operation ▯ is used for ______.
   (A) Adding or changing border around a page
   (B) Choose a color background for page
   (C) Merge cells
   (D) Table properties

3. ______ is the maximum number of columns that can be inserted in a table in a MS Word document.
   (A) 35 (B) 15
   (C) 63 (D) 65

4. When you click Distribute Rows, it distributes the __________.
   (A) Height of the selected rows equally between them
   (B) Width of the selected rows equally between them
   (C) Header in the table
   (D) Width of the selected columns equally between them

5. In Table Tools, under Design tab, by shading you can ________.
   (A) Specify a color for page background
   (B) Specify a color for the background behind the selected text or paragraph
   (C) Highlight the text
   (D) Highlight the border of the selected cell in a table

6. You have been editing an existing letter in MS Word. You want to review the modifications to the letter since you last edited it, before you finally print it. Which feature of MS Word should you be using?
   (A) AutoSummarize
   (B) Compare and Merge documents
   (C) Track changes
   (D) Mail Merge Wizard

7. How do you increase the line spacing between two lines?
   (A) Home Tab → Insert → Line Spacing
   (B) Home Tab → Paragraph → Line and Paragraph Spacing
   (C) Insert Tab → Insert → Line Spacing
   (D) Insert Tab → Paragraph → Line Spacing

8. In newspaper column format, what is the minimum width of a column?
   (A) 0.25"   (B) 0.5"
   (C) 1.0"   (D) 1.5"

9. You can go to the Insert columns dialog box by _______.
   (A) Clicking Columns in the Insert card
   (B) Pressing Alt + O + C
   (C) Clicking Columns in page Setup of page Layout tab
   (D) Both (b) and (c)

10. The maximum size that you can specify for a font is _______ points.
    (A) 72   (B) 1638
    (C) 16038   (D) 68

11. Turabian and GB7714 are types of _______ styles.
    (A) Text
    (B) Cross Reference
    (C) Footnote
    (D) Citation

12. How can you change a page number style from 1, 2, 3 _______ to a, b, c _______?
    (A) Click page Layout → Header & Footer → Page Number → Format Page Numbers
    (B) Click Format → Header & Footer → Page Number → Format Page Numbers
    (C) Click Insert → Header & Footer → Page Number → Format Page Numbers
    (D) None of these

13. This button AB^1 is used to _______.
    (A) Insert a footnote
    (B) Format the selected text as uppercase
    (C) Format the selected text as superscript
    (D) Insert an endnote

14. Shortcut key to insert endnote text is _______.
    (A) Alt + Ctrl + E   (B) Alt + Ctrl + M
    (C) Alt + Ctrl + N   (D) Alt + Ctrl + D

15. You can choose settings for features like dictionary, proofing and language when you _______.
    (A) Click on the Tools Tab, click Options.
    (B) Click on the File Tab, click Word Options.
    (C) Right-click anywhere on the ribbon and choose Options.
    (D) Click on the View tab, click Properties.

16. Match the following.

Column - I	Column - II
(i) .docx	(a) A Word template with no macros or code.
(ii) .dotx	(b) A Word document that could contain macros or code.
(iii) .docm	(c) A standard Word document with no macros or code.
(iv) .dotm	(d) A Word template that could contain macros or code.

    (A) (i) – (c),(ii) – (a), (iii) – (d), (iv) – (b)
    (B) (i) – (c), (ii) – (a), (iii) – (b), (iv) – (d)
    (C) (i) – (a), (ii) – (c), (iii) – (b), (iv) – (d)
    (D) (i) – (b), (ii) – (d), (iii) – (c), (iv) – (a)

17. _______ automatically adjusts the amount of space between certain characters of a word typed in a font like Times New Roman, so that the entire word looks more evenly spaced.
    (A) Kerning   (B) Spacing
    (C) Scaling   (D) Positioning

18. **A**n Operating System acts as intermediate between the user and the machine.

    (A) WordArt
    (B) Footnotes
    (C) Drop Cap
    (D) Tab Stop

19. For Mail Merge in MS Word, ______ consists of names and addresses to be printed on labels and envelopes.
  (A) Data source   (B) Main document
  (C) New document   (D) Web site

20. The ________________ tab appears when we insert a picture in the word document.
  (A) Insert picture   (B) Format
  (C) Shapes   (D) Clip Art

HOTS (ACHIEVERS SECTION)

21. Shraddha is making a document in MS Word and now she wants to insert an image, and she also wants that whatever changes she makes to secure of image shall reflect in Word also. However, she does not want that if the original file is deleted, the image from word document also gets deleted. Which of the following options she should select?
  (A) Insert tab → illustrations group → Picture → click Insert in Insert Picture dialog box.
  (B) Insert tab → illustrations group → Picture → click Link to file in Insert picture dialog box.
  (C) Insert tab → illustrations group → Picture → click Insert and Link in Insert Picture dialog box.
  (D) Insert tab → illustrations group → Picture → Double click on the image.

22. What is the other way to select the entire document rather than pressing Ctrl + A in MS Word?
  (A) Triple click in the right margin when the pointer's shape is the arrow.
  (B) Triple click in the left margin when the pointer's shape is the arrow.
  (C) Triple click inside a paragraph.
  (D) Triple click anywhere in the document.

23. The Footnote Text style defines characters as ________________.
  (A) 12-point Times New Roman and paragraphs as single-spaced and right-aligned
  (B) 10-point Times New Roman and paragraphs as double-spaced and left-aligned
  (C) 12-point Times New Roman and paragraphs as double-spaced and right-aligned
  (D) 10-point Times New Roman and paragraphs as single-spaced and left-aligned

24. The ____________ in the Resume Wizard dialog box indicates the wizard is ready to create the document.
  (A) Start panel
  (B) Address panel
  (C) Add/Sort Heading panel
  (D) Finish panel

25. The spike ________________.
  (A) Allows you to combine text from several documents and then insert all the text into one document at one time
  (B) Allows you to edit auto text entries
  (C) Allows you to format auto text entries
  (D) All of these

—Darken Your Choice with HB Pencil—

1. Ⓐ Ⓑ Ⓒ Ⓓ	6. Ⓐ Ⓑ Ⓒ Ⓓ	11. Ⓐ Ⓑ Ⓒ Ⓓ	16. Ⓐ Ⓑ Ⓒ Ⓓ	21. Ⓐ Ⓑ Ⓒ Ⓓ
2. Ⓐ Ⓑ Ⓒ Ⓓ	7. Ⓐ Ⓑ Ⓒ Ⓓ	12. Ⓐ Ⓑ Ⓒ Ⓓ	17. Ⓐ Ⓑ Ⓒ Ⓓ	22. Ⓐ Ⓑ Ⓒ Ⓓ
3. Ⓐ Ⓑ Ⓒ Ⓓ	8. Ⓐ Ⓑ Ⓒ Ⓓ	13. Ⓐ Ⓑ Ⓒ Ⓓ	18. Ⓐ Ⓑ Ⓒ Ⓓ	23. Ⓐ Ⓑ Ⓒ Ⓓ
4. Ⓐ Ⓑ Ⓒ Ⓓ	9. Ⓐ Ⓑ Ⓒ Ⓓ	14. Ⓐ Ⓑ Ⓒ Ⓓ	19. Ⓐ Ⓑ Ⓒ Ⓓ	24. Ⓐ Ⓑ Ⓒ Ⓓ
5. Ⓐ Ⓑ Ⓒ Ⓓ	10. Ⓐ Ⓑ Ⓒ Ⓓ	15. Ⓐ Ⓑ Ⓒ Ⓓ	20. Ⓐ Ⓑ Ⓒ Ⓓ	25. Ⓐ Ⓑ Ⓒ Ⓓ

OLYMPIAD WORKBOOK (NCO) CLASS– 7

MS POWERPOINT

LEARNING OBJECTIVES

➤ Fundamentals of MS PowerPoint
➤ Slide master and theme

MULTIPLE CHOICE QUESTIONS

1. The File tab menu and _______ view contain commands for working with a program's files including New, Open, Save etc.
   (A) Normal View
   (B) Backstage View
   (C) Slide View
   (D) None of these

2. _______ is not present in Design tab.
   (A) Page Setup
   (B) Background Styles
   (C) Slide Orientation
   (D) Rehearse Timings

3. To automatically place your school logo at the same position on every slide, you should insert the school logo on the _______.
   (A) Handout master   (B) Notes master
   (C) Slide master   (D) All of these

4. Use the _______ tab, to insert an image to your presentation.
   (A) Home   (B) Design
   (C) Insert   (D) All of these

5. In slide show view, the movement that you see when one slide changes to another is called a _______.
   (A) Transition   (B) Animation
   (C) Fade   (D) View

6. To correct a spelling error found in spell check, _______ on the misspelled word.
   (A) Double click
   (B) Hover over
   (C) Right click
   (D) None of these

7. _______ is generally the first slide of the presentation. It is used to introduce a topic and set the tone for the presentation.
   (A) Table slide   (B) Graph slide
   (C) Bullet slide   (D) Title slide

8. Select the _______ view at the bottom of the PowerPoint window to present your presentation.
   (A) 🖳   (B) 🖵
   (C) 🔲   (D) 📖

9. The print pane in the Backstage view can _______.
   (A) Adjust the page orientation
   (B) View the print preview
   (C) Print your presentation
   (D) All of these

10. _______ is not a transition effect.
    (A) Blinks diagonal   (B) Dissolve
    (C) Fade   (D) Blinds

11. Given below are a few actions. Which of the following can you assign to a slide object or an action button?
 (A) Run a macro (B) Play a sound
 (C) Hyperlink (D) All of these

12. You can change a bullet's ______.
 (A) Color (B) Size
 (C) Shape (D) All of these

13. When you hide a slide, the hidden slide ______.
 (A) Is not displayed in the slide show
 (B) Is deleted
 (C) Content is hidden, and a blank slide is displayed in lieu
 (D) Contents are deleted

14. A multi-hierarchical list is also called a ______.
 (A) Multilevel list (B) Animated list
 (C) Distributed list (D) Tracked list

15. When the Draw Table feature is selected, the mouse pointer appears as a ______.
 (A) Solid plus sign (B) Solid arrow
 (C) I-beam (D) Pencil

16. The brightness and contrast of an image can be adjusted using the ______ command.
 (A) Color
 (B) Compress Pictures
 (C) Corrections
 (D) Crop

17. To add shadow to a shape, use the ______ tool.
 (A) Shape Fill
 (B) Shape Outline
 (C) Shape Effects
 (D) Send Backwards

18. To display a context on a slide, ______.
 (A) Click the shortcut button on the Home Tab
 (B) Right click on the current slide
 (C) Click an object on the current slide
 (D) All of these

19. When text in a placeholder does not fit in one slide, you can split Text Between Two slides by using the __________ that appears when the slide is filled.
 (A) Auto Fit Options Button
 (B) Split Slide Option Button
 (C) Distribute Text Option Button
 (D) Format slide Option Button

20. ______ is not a type of an animation effect.
 (A) Entrance
 (B) Equation
 (C) Emphasis
 (D) Exit

HOTS (ACHIEVERS SECTION)

21. In MS PowerPoint, when the insertion point is flashing in a box, what should be pressed to select the text box itself?
 (A) Alt
 (B) Esc
 (C) Ctrl
 (D) Alt + Ctrl

22. While making a presentation in MS-Power Point, Sheetal has set different slide timing on individual slides. Now she wants to check the timing of slide, which view is the best for the purpose?

 (A)   (B)

 (C)   (D)

23. In normal view, how can you quickly change to handout master view?
   (A) Click the outline tab and select handout master view
   (B) Press the shift key and click the handout master view button
   (C) On the view menu, click slide sorter, and click handouts.
   (D) Ctrl + F11

24. How can you quickly reinstate a deleted footer placeholder in master view?

   (A) Re-apply the slide layout
   (B) Create a new slide master
   (C) Re-apply the footer placeholder
   (D) Reinsert the slide

25. Which of the following allows you to select more than one slide in a presentation?
   (A) Ctrl + Click each slide
   (B) Shift + Click each slide
   (C) Alt + Click each slide
   (D) Shift + drag each slide

MS EXCEL

LEARNING OBJECTIVES

- ➤ Basics of MS Excel
- ➤ Functions and formulas in MS Excel
- ➤ Working in MS Excel
- ➤ Macros and Charts in Excel

MULTIPLE CHOICE QUESTIONS

1. A row column arrangement of data, and the formulas to manipulate it is called a ______.
   (A) Spreadsheet   (B) Table sheet
   (C) Grid sheet   (D) Role sheet

2. Where is the address of the active cell displayed in an active worksheet?
   (A) Row heading
   (B) Status Bar
   (C) Name Box
   (D) Formula Box

3. Current date and time in a cell can be entered using the formula ______.
   (A) = TODAY( )
   (B) = NOW ()
   (C) = TIME ()
   (D) = CURRENTTIME ()

4. $\sum$ is ______.
   (A) The Auto Correct button
   (B) The Auto Format button
   (C) The Auto Sum button
   (D) The conditional format button

5. The error value # NULL! appears in a cell because ______.
   (A) The formula is trying to multiply a value

   (B) The formula refers to a cell that is not valid
   (C) The formula uses an intersection of two ranges that do not intersect
   (D) The formula is trying to divide by Zero

6. When applying conditional formatting to a cell, you can compare the conditions against ______.
   (A) Cell value
   (B) Applied formula
   (C) Both (a) and (b)
   (D) None of these

7. Paper spreadsheets can have all advantages of electronic spreadsheets except ______.
   (A) Rows and Columns
   (B) Headings
   (C) Speed and Accuracy
   (D) None of these

8. Which of the following is NOT present is insert tab?
   (A) [A]   (B) [image]
   (C) Ω (D) AA

9. In MS Excel, hyperlinks can be ______.
    (A) Special shapes like stars and banners
    (B) Drawing objects like rectangles, ovals
    (C) Text and pictures
    (D) All of these

10. Which of the following is a valid cell range?
    (A) A1
    (B) A1-C4
    (C) A1:C4
    (D) C4:A1

11. With the formula bar active, you can see ____________.
    (A) The Insert Function button
    (B) The Cancel button
    (C) The Enter button
    (D) All of these

12. The function of the given icon is ______.

    (A) To add a new row
    (B) To create subtotals
    (C) To insert a new function
    (D) To create a sum function

13. Which of these is not an MS Excel valid function?
    (A) COUNTIF
    (B) SUMIF
    (C) COUNTA
    (D) COUNTUP

14. Identify the given icon.

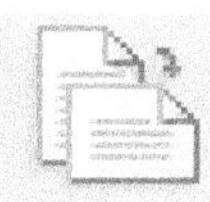

    (A) Orientation
    (B) Text Direction
    (C) Decrease Indent
    (D) Wrap Text

15. What is the most appropriate formula you can put in the cell B2 to calculate a 9% tax, if value in A2 is 73745.98?
    (A) =A2*0.09
    (B) =A2*0.09%
    (C) =A2*1. 09
    (D) =A2+(A2*0.09)

16. If the current cell shows the results of a formula, what key should be pressed so that the actual formula is displayed in the cell?
    (A) F1
    (B) F2
    (C) F3
    (D) F4

17. A '$' sign in a cell reference like in A1 means that ______.
    (A) The cell reference is relative
    (B) The cell is formatted to dollars.
    (C) The cell reference is absolute.
    (D) The cell reference is invalid.

18. Why should you select this button?

    (A) To get external data form an existing source.
    (B) To get external data from text.
    (C) To get external data from other sources.
    (D) To get external data from the web.

19. The first step while creating a formula for a cell is ____________.
    (A) Select the cell you want to place the formula into.
    (B) Type the equals sign (=) to tell Excel that you're about to enter a formula.
    (C) Enter the formula using any input values and the appropriate mathematical operators that make up your formula.
    (D) Choose the new command from the file menu.

20. The formula 'NETWORKDAYS' is used to return the ______.
    (A) Network of days
    (B) Number of whole workdays between two dates
    (C) Number of months in a year
    (D) Number of days a person worked in Excel

21. In MS Excel 2010, what would be the result of the formula given below?

    =SUM(CHOOSE(2, A1:A10, B1:B10, C1:C10)

    (A) It will show the second largest sum.
    (B) It will add the value in the range B1:B10
    (C) It will add the value in the first two ranges.
    (D) It will add the value in the range C1:C10.

22. The keyboard shortcut to scroll the screen so that active cell is visible in MS Excel is _______.

    (A) Ctrl + Backspace   (B) Ctrl + O
    (C) Alt + Backspace   (D) Ctrl + Spacebar

23. Which of the following is correct description of Auto Complete feature of MS Excel?

    (A) It will force MS Excel to display value in multiple lines within the cell.
    (B) It automatically fills the entry based on other entries that you already made in column, when you type the first few letters of a text.
    (C) It inserts a series of values or text items in a range of cells.
    (D) None of these

24. Which of the following methods is not used to enter data in the cell?

    (A) Press Esc
    (B) Press Tab
    (C) Press Enter
    (D) Use any arrow key

25. How will you merge a range of cells?

    (A) Ctrl + Shift + M
    (B) Ctrl + M
    (C) Select the cells you want to merge and right click and select format cell
    (D) Select the cells you want to merge, and select Merge cells options.

1.	A B C D	6.	A B C D	11.	A B C D	16.	A B C D	21.	A B C D
2.	A B C D	7.	A B C D	12.	A B C D	17.	A B C D	22.	A B C D
3.	A B C D	8.	A B C D	13.	A B C D	18.	A B C D	23.	A B C D
4.	A B C D	9.	A B C D	14.	A B C D	19.	A B C D	24.	A B C D
5.	A B C D	10.	A B C D	15.	A B C D	20.	A B C D	25.	A B C D

PROGRAMMING IN QBASIC

LEARNING OBJECTIVES

➤ Basics of QBasic

MULTIPLE CHOICE QUESTIONS

1. What is the group instructions directing a computer called?
   (A) Storage
   (B) Memory
   (C) Logic
   (D) Program

2. What is the full form of BASIC?
   (A) Beginners All Purpose Symbolic Instruction Code
   (A) Basic All program Symbolic Integrated Computer
   (C) Basic All proper Symbolic Insert Code
   (D) Basic All print Syntax Instruction Code

3. Which of the following is the file name of QBASIC program?
   (A) QBasic.exe
   (B) QBASIC.doc
   (C) QBasic.ppt
   (D) QBASIC.xis

4. BASIC was developed in the year __________.
   (A) 1964
   (B) 1966
   (C) 1968
   (D) 1962

5. What is the shortcut key to run a QBASIC program?
   (A) Alt + F9
   (B) Alt + F5
   (C) Shift + F5
   (D) Shift + F9

6. If the QBASIC window fills the entire screen, you can press __________ to make it smaller?
   (A) Alt + Enter
   (B) Alt + Esc
   (C) Alt + Fa
   (D) Alt + F5

7. In BASIC language, what are the values which do not change during the execution of program?
   (A) Variables
   (B) Constants
   (C) Operators
   (D) Error

8. How are the string constants represented?
   (A) They are enclosed in a double quotation mark
   (B) They are enclosed in a single quotation mark
   (C) They are enclosed in square brackets
   (D) They are enclosed in parentheses

9. Which of the following is an INVALID representation of constants in QBASIC language?
    (A) "Hello"
    (B) "16/10/2005"
    (C) 0.742
    (D) "Q"BASIC"

10. In QBASIC language, what are the quantities which change values during the execution of a program?
    (A) Variables
    (B) Constants
    (C) Errors
    (D) Operators

11. String variables must end with a ______ sign?
    (A) S
    (B) +
    (C) −
    (D) @

12. Which of the following is an INVALID numeric variable?
    (A) T24
    (B) A
    (C) M2
    (D) 2B43

13. Which of the following is a string variable?
    (A) PS
    (B) M2
    (C) OB
    (D) TITLE

14. Which of the following are relational operators?
    (A) *
    (B) ^
    (C) AND
    (D) <>

15. What are instructions in QBASIC called?

    (A) Operators
    (B) Programs
    (C) Statement
    (D) String

16. What is the input command for string values?
    (A) INPUT P
    (B) INPUT P$
    (C) INPUT $P
    (D) INPUT "P"

17. Which command is used to clear the screen of QBASIC windows?
    (A) REM
    (B) NOT
    (C) CLR
    (D) CLS

18. What will the given command do?
    LET C = A + B
    (A) The string variable C receives the value of A + B
    (B) The numerical valuable C is assigned the value of A + B
    (C) The string variable C is assigned the expression A + B
    (D) An error message is displayed

19. What is the output of the given program?
    10 INPUT "Enter your favorite subject" 20 END
    (A) Computer
    (B) Favorite
    (C) Subject =
    (D) Enter your favorite subject

20. Which statement is used for writing comments in the QBASIC program?
    (A) LET
    (B) REM
    (C) INPUT
    (D) PRINT

21. What will be output of the given QBASIC code?

Code A	Code B
FOR 1 = 1 TO 5	FOR 1 = 1 TO 5
STEP 2	STEP 1
PRINT 1	PRINT 1
NEXT 1	I = I + 1 NEXT 1

(A) Both will print
1
2
3

(B)
Code A	Code B
1	1
3	2
5	3
	4
	5

(C)
Code A	Code B
1	1
3	2
5	4

(D)
Code A	Code B
1	1
2	3
3	5
4	
5	

22. What is the correct QBASIC code to set the whole background to be red and foreground color to be yellow?

(A) COLOR 6, 14
   PRINT "This text is yellow over Red"

(B) COLOR 14, 4
   CLS
   PRINT "This text is yellow over Red"

(C) COLOR 4, 14
   PRINT "This text is yellow over Red"

(D) COLOR 4,14
   CLS
   PRINT "This text is yellow over Red"

23. It consists of sequence of characters which must be enclosed by quotation mark. It is known as _______?
(A) Numeric Variable
(B) Numeric Constant
(C) String Variable
(D) String Constant

24. Which of the following is not a reserved word or contain a space?
(A) Numbers   (B) Strings
(C) Constants   (D) Variable

25. These are formed from the character of the Qbasic character set. They are known as?
(A) Reserved Word   (B) Variable
(C) Constants   (D) Numbers

—Darken Your Choice with HB Pencil—

1. Ⓐ Ⓑ Ⓒ Ⓓ	6. Ⓐ Ⓑ Ⓒ Ⓓ	11. Ⓐ Ⓑ Ⓒ Ⓓ	16. Ⓐ Ⓑ Ⓒ Ⓓ	21. Ⓐ Ⓑ Ⓒ Ⓓ
2. Ⓐ Ⓑ Ⓒ Ⓓ	7. Ⓐ Ⓑ Ⓒ Ⓓ	12. Ⓐ Ⓑ Ⓒ Ⓓ	17. Ⓐ Ⓑ Ⓒ Ⓓ	22. Ⓐ Ⓑ Ⓒ Ⓓ
3. Ⓐ Ⓑ Ⓒ Ⓓ	8. Ⓐ Ⓑ Ⓒ Ⓓ	13. Ⓐ Ⓑ Ⓒ Ⓓ	18. Ⓐ Ⓑ Ⓒ Ⓓ	23. Ⓐ Ⓑ Ⓒ Ⓓ
4. Ⓐ Ⓑ Ⓒ Ⓓ	9. Ⓐ Ⓑ Ⓒ Ⓓ	14. Ⓐ Ⓑ Ⓒ Ⓓ	19. Ⓐ Ⓑ Ⓒ Ⓓ	24. Ⓐ Ⓑ Ⓒ Ⓓ
5. Ⓐ Ⓑ Ⓒ Ⓓ	10. Ⓐ Ⓑ Ⓒ Ⓓ	15. Ⓐ Ⓑ Ⓒ Ⓓ	20. Ⓐ Ⓑ Ⓒ Ⓓ	25. Ⓐ Ⓑ Ⓒ Ⓓ

LEARNING OBJECTIVES

➤ Internet Explorer
➤ Internet safety

MULTIPLE CHOICE QUESTIONS

1. Find the odd one out.
   (A) www.blogger.com
   (B) www.tumblr.com
   (C) www.blogspot.com
   (D) www.google.com

2. Identify this internet tool.
   It is used for locating information on the internet. It matches search terms with indexed pages.
   (A) Database
   (B) Deep Web
   (C) URL
   (D) Search Engine

3. You cannot browse websites on the internet using _______.
   (A) Broadband
   (B) Dial-up
   (C) 3G/4G
   (D) FTP

4. Which of the following is the use of the internet?
   (A) Software sharing
   (B) Organization promotion
   (C) On-line shopping
   (D) All of these

5. _______ is a program that is used to access various internet resources.
   (A) Address
   (B) Browser
   (C) Provider
   (D) Protocol

6. _______ is authoring/maintaining/adding/ updating articles to an existing blog.
   (A) Weblog
   (B) Blogging
   (C) Links
   (D) Forum

7. Internet _______ are like 24-hour coffee shops with people eager to communicate anytime they want.
   (A) Online libraries
   (B) Chat room
   (C) Electronic post offices
   (D) Blogs

8. _______ is a program that may interrupt the normal operation of a computer.
   (A) Routine
   (B) Disabler
   (C) Virus
   (D) Destroyer

9. ______ is/are phase of a virus.
   (A) Infection
   (B) Attack
   (C) Both (a) and (B)
   (D) None of these

10. Which of the following statements is true for a Boot Virus?
    (A) It infects boot/master boot records on a hard disk.
    (B) It is the most active while a computer is booting
    (C) Disk killer is a well known boot virus
    (D) All of these

11. Which of the following statements is true for a program Files virus?
    (A) It infects executable/program files like .exe and .com
    (B) It is loaded in memory as soon as the program executes.
    (C) Sunday virus is a type of Program file virus.
    (D) All of these

12. To identify, prevent, quarantine and remove viruses, you need a ______ software.
    (A) Clean virus   (B) Antivirus
    (C) Remove virus   (D) None of these

13. To prevent virus from infecting your computer, you should ______.
    (A) Equip your PC with a licensed antivirus program
    (B) Scan flash drives and floppy disks before copying data from them
    (C) Not install pirated software from unknown sources on your computer
    (D) All of these

14. Identify the following.
    It is software program.
    It monitors a user's computing habits.
    It records user's personal information.
    It sends the recorded information to third parties without the user's knowledge.
    (A) Spyware   (B) Adware
    (C) Malware   (D) None of these

15. What is the process of sending message from one person to another person via computer called?
    (A) Email   (B) SMS
    (C) Advertisement   (D) Marketing

16. What does ISP stand for?
    (A) Internet Service Provider
    (B) Information Service Provider
    (C) Internet Service Program
    (D) Information Service Program

17. E-mail has become one of the fastest messaging services. What does e-mail stand for?
    (A) Electrical Mail
    (B) Electronic Mail
    (C) Energetic Mail
    (D) Emergency Mail

18. Which of the following is the first page of website?
    (A) Home page
    (B) Web page
    (C) Relative page
    (D) Previous page

19. What is the full form of DNS?
    (A) Data Numbering Service
    (B) Device Networking System
    (C) Domain Naming System
    (D) Data Naming Service

20. Match the following.

Abbreviation	Stands for
1. .com	P. Education
2. .edu	Q. India
3. .in	R. Australia
4. .au	S. Commercial

    (A) 1P, 2Q, 3R, 4S   (B) 1Q, 2R, 3S,4P
    (C) 1R, 2S, 3P, 4Q   (D) 1S, 2P, 3Q, 4R

21. Jyoti has installed some programs from Windows Live at the end of the download and install process, the Window Live installer is asking for Windows Live ID. In which of the following cases she doesn't already have a Windows Live ID?
    (A) If she uses Hotmail
    (B) If she uses Xbox Live
    (C) If she uses Gmail
    (D) If she uses Windows Live Messenger

22. Before downloading which package can be downloaded through internet for testing purpose?
    (A) Shareware
    (B) Pirated Software
    (C) Backup Copy
    (D) Beta Software

23. Based on the packet's address, the device that has been designed to forward packets to specific ports is?
    (A) Speciality Hub
    (B) Filtering Hub
    (C) Switching Hub
    (D) Port Hub

24. _________ topology is not of a broadcast type?
    (A) Bus   (B) Ring
    (C) Mesh   (D) Star

25. IP is defined in-
    (A) RFC 790   (B) RFC 791
    (C) RFC 792   (D) RFC 793

Darken Your Choice with HB Pencil

1. Ⓐ Ⓑ Ⓒ Ⓓ	6. Ⓐ Ⓑ Ⓒ Ⓓ	11. Ⓐ Ⓑ Ⓒ Ⓓ	16. Ⓐ Ⓑ Ⓒ Ⓓ	21. Ⓐ Ⓑ Ⓒ Ⓓ
2. Ⓐ Ⓑ Ⓒ Ⓓ	7. Ⓐ Ⓑ Ⓒ Ⓓ	12. Ⓐ Ⓑ Ⓒ Ⓓ	17. Ⓐ Ⓑ Ⓒ Ⓓ	22. Ⓐ Ⓑ Ⓒ Ⓓ
3. Ⓐ Ⓑ Ⓒ Ⓓ	8. Ⓐ Ⓑ Ⓒ Ⓓ	13. Ⓐ Ⓑ Ⓒ Ⓓ	18. Ⓐ Ⓑ Ⓒ Ⓓ	23. Ⓐ Ⓑ Ⓒ Ⓓ
4. Ⓐ Ⓑ Ⓒ Ⓓ	9. Ⓐ Ⓑ Ⓒ Ⓓ	14. Ⓐ Ⓑ Ⓒ Ⓓ	19. Ⓐ Ⓑ Ⓒ Ⓓ	24. Ⓐ Ⓑ Ⓒ Ⓓ
5. Ⓐ Ⓑ Ⓒ Ⓓ	10. Ⓐ Ⓑ Ⓒ Ⓓ	15. Ⓐ Ⓑ Ⓒ Ⓓ	20. Ⓐ Ⓑ Ⓒ Ⓓ	25. Ⓐ Ⓑ Ⓒ Ⓓ

NETWORKING

LEARNING OBJECTIVES

- ➤ Need of Computer network
- ➤ Types of Network
- ➤ IP Address
- ➤ Network topology

MULTIPLE CHOICE QUESTIONS

1. Which of the following is not a type of Computer Network?
   (A) Local Area Network (LAN)
   (B) Personal Area Network (PAN)
   (C) Remote Area Network (RAN)
   (D) Metropolitan Area Network (MAN)

2. What is the full Form of NIC?
   (A) New Internet Connection
   (B) Network Interface Card
   (C) Network Interface Connection
   (D) Net Interface Card

3. Star Topology is based on a central device that can be __________?
   (A) Hub
   (B) Switch
   (C) Only (A)
   (D) Both (A) and (B)

4. Which topology requires a central controller or hub?
   (A) Star
   (B) Bus
   (C) Ring
   (D) None of these

5. Which topology requires a multipoint connection?
   (A) Star
   (B) Bus
   (C) Ring
   (D) None of these

6. This was the first network.
   (A) CSNET
   (B) NSFNET
   (C) ANSNET
   (D) ARPANET

7. __________ refers to the physical or logical arrangement of a network.
   (A) Data flow
   (B) Mode of operation
   (C) Topology
   (D) None of these

8. Devices can be arranged in a _____ topology.
   (A) star
   (B) ring
   (C) bus
   (D) all of these

9. A _______ is a data communication system within a building, or campus, or between nearby buildings.
   (A) MAN
   (B) LAN
   (C) WAN
   (D) None of these

10. A _______ is a data communication system spanning states, countries, or the whole world.
    (A) MAN
    (B) LAN
    (C) WAN
    (D) None of these

11. _______ is a collection of many separate networks.
    (A) WAN
    (B) Internet
    (C) LAN
    (D) None of these

12. A _______ is a set of rules that governs data communication.
    (A) Forum
    (B) Protocol
    (C) Standard
    (D) None of these

13. The device, which converts digital signal into analog, and the vice versa, is known as:
    (A) Modem
    (B) Modulator
    (C) Generator
    (D) Analogue

14. Which is the most popular and commonly used LAN (Local Area Network) protocol?
   (A) Ethernet   (B) Internet
   (C) Relay   (D) LANR

15. WAP stands for
   (A) Wired Application Protocol
   (B) Wireless Analog Protocol
   (C) Wireless Application Protocol
   (D) Wired Analog Protocol

16. Interconnection of various computer systems located atdifferent places is known as:
   (A) Connectors   (B) Network
   (C) Internet   (D) None of these

17. LAN stands for
   (A) Logical Area Network
   (B) Low Area Network
   (C) Loaded Area Network
   (D) Local Area Network

18. Which of these is not a type of network?
   (A) LAN   (B) BAN
   (C) SAN   (D) MAN

19. Which network is also known as Server Area Network?
   (A) Storage Area Network
   (B) Client Area Network
   (C) Workstation Area Network
   (D) Distributed Area Network

20. Which of the following technique is used by VPN?
   (A) Tunneling   (B) Multiplexing
   (C) Cascading   (D) Switching

HOTS (ACHIEVERS SECTION)

21. Which of these is a standard interface for serial data transmission?
   (A) ASCII   (B) RS232C
   (C) 2   (D) Centronics

22. Which type of topology is best suited for large businesses which must carefully control and coordinate the operation of distributed branch outlets?
   (A) Ring   (B) Local area
   (C) Hierarchical (D) Star

23. Which of the following transmission directions listed is not a legitimate channel?
   (A) Simplex   (B) Half Duplex
   (C) Full Duplex (D) Double Duplex

24. "Parity bits" are used for which of the following purposes?
   (A) Encryption of data
   (B) To transmit faster
   (C) To detect errors
   (D) To identify the user

25. What kind of transmission medium is most appropriate to carry data in a computer network that is exposed to electrical interferences?
   (A) Unshielded twisted pair
   (B) Optical fiber
   (C) Coaxial cable
   (D) Microwave

––––––– Darken Your Choice with HB Pencil –––––––

1.	Ⓐ Ⓑ Ⓒ Ⓓ	6.	Ⓐ Ⓑ Ⓒ Ⓓ	11.	Ⓐ Ⓑ Ⓒ Ⓓ	16.	Ⓐ Ⓑ Ⓒ Ⓓ	21.	Ⓐ Ⓑ Ⓒ Ⓓ
2.	Ⓐ Ⓑ Ⓒ Ⓓ	7.	Ⓐ Ⓑ Ⓒ Ⓓ	12.	Ⓐ Ⓑ Ⓒ Ⓓ	17.	Ⓐ Ⓑ Ⓒ Ⓓ	22.	Ⓐ Ⓑ Ⓒ Ⓓ
3.	Ⓐ Ⓑ Ⓒ Ⓓ	8.	Ⓐ Ⓑ Ⓒ Ⓓ	13.	Ⓐ Ⓑ Ⓒ Ⓓ	18.	Ⓐ Ⓑ Ⓒ Ⓓ	23.	Ⓐ Ⓑ Ⓒ Ⓓ
4.	Ⓐ Ⓑ Ⓒ Ⓓ	9.	Ⓐ Ⓑ Ⓒ Ⓓ	14.	Ⓐ Ⓑ Ⓒ Ⓓ	19.	Ⓐ Ⓑ Ⓒ Ⓓ	24.	Ⓐ Ⓑ Ⓒ Ⓓ
5.	Ⓐ Ⓑ Ⓒ Ⓓ	10.	Ⓐ Ⓑ Ⓒ Ⓓ	15.	Ⓐ Ⓑ Ⓒ Ⓓ	20.	Ⓐ Ⓑ Ⓒ Ⓓ	25.	Ⓐ Ⓑ Ⓒ Ⓓ

LATEST DEVELOPMENTS IN 'IT' 

LEARNING OBJECTIVES

➤ Some of the latest development in the field of IT

MULTIPLE CHOICE QUESTIONS

1. In computer terminology, which of the following statements define a Dorkbot?
   - (A) A family of malware worms.
   - (B) Dorkbot typically spreads through instant messaging and USB removable drives.
   - (C) Dorkbot spreads through social media channels like Facebook and Twitter.
   - (D) All of these

2. A Botnet is a ______.
   - (A) Type of bot running on smart phones, attempting to gain complete control of the device
   - (B) Type of bot running on an IRC network and created by a Trojan
   - (C) SMC attack
   - (D) Mobile VoIP

3. Barcrafts are centred on what video game?
   - (A) Mine craft
   - (B) World of warcraft
   - (C) War craft III
   - (D) Star craft II

4. Which of the following is the most widespread Botnet in history?
   - (A) Hekaton
   - (B) Dorkbot
   - (C) Ransomware
   - (D) Zeus

5. What is an Instagram?
   - (A) An android app that let you store your photo and videos.
   - (B) It supports various built-in filter effect.
   - (C) Allows instant sharing on facebook, twitter, flicker and Tumblr.
   - (D) All of these

6. Which of the following is the latest release of Samsung's popular Galaxy smart phone unveiled in February 2023?
   - (A) Samsung Galaxy Tab
   - (B) Samsung Galaxy S4
   - (C) Samsung Galaxy S6
   - (D) Samsung Galaxy S23

7. Which of the following is a windows notebook with a lid that pops off to become a standalone state?
   - (A) HP Essential
   - (B) HP Probook
   - (C) HP Envy x2 Hybrid PC
   - (D) HP Elite Book

8. What is the name of the feature in Mac OS X that displays a tray of icons?
   (A) File Vault (B) Dock
   (C) Mission control (D) Spotlight

9. The latest touch series of notebooks from ASUS are called ______.
   (A) Lamborghini
   (B) Taichi
   (C) Vivo Book
   (D) Transformer Book

10. Which of the following is not present in iphone?
    (A) Multitouch (B) Edge
    (C) ios6 (D) Radio

11. The list shows new and changed features of OSX Mavericks.
    (i) icloud keychain Sync
    (ii) Added new ibook application
    (iii) App Nap
    (iv) SMB 4 is the default protocol for sharing files
    Which of the following features are true?
    (A) (i), (ii), (iv)
    (B) Both (ii) and (iii)
    (C) Only (iv)
    (D) (i), (ii), and (iii)

12. What is Pinterest?
    (A) A pinboard-style photo sharing website that allows user to create and manage theme based image collection.
    (B) A pinboard-style Bookmark website that allows user to track favourites.
    (C) Social news and entertainment website where users submit content in the form of pinboards.
    (D) An interesting note-taking site.

13. Video glasses are also knows as ______.
    (A) Head mounted display
    (B) Personal media viewers
    (C) Google Goggle
    (D) Both (A) and (B)

14. Which of the following is basically an impression of depth and is used to describe the brain's ability to put separate images together in order to form one 3-D image?
    (A) Stereopsis
    (B) Binocular fusion
    (C) Binocular disparity
    (D) Strabismus

15. Identify the following:
    It is an online social networking service and micro blogging service.
    Its users can send and read text based messages of up to 140 characters called tweets.
    It was created by Jack Dorsey in March 2006.
    (A) Facebook (B) Twitter
    (C) Linked in (D) YAHOO

16. GPS devices can pinpoint locations by ______.
    (A) Satellites
    (B) Lasers
    (C) Radioactive Waves
    (D) All of these

17. Which hugely popular Nintendo 64 game was rumoured to have a secret location accessible in its very first level?
    (A) Golden Eye 007
    (B) Mario 64
    (C) The legend of Zelda: Ocarina of time
    (D) The prince of Persia

18. The Black phone runs on which version of Android?
    (A) PrivatOS (B) Kitkat
    (C) Honey comb (D) Jelly Bean

19. Semantic Web term was coined by ______.
    (A) Jack Dorsey
    (B) Tim Berners-Lee
    (C) Dick Costolo
    (D) Noah Glass

20. Altec Lansing V2621 is a model name for
    a _______.
    (A) Graphics Card
    (B) Speaker
    (C) Optical Drive
    (D) Sound Card

HOTS (ACHIEVERS SECTION)

21. Select the correct statement about the given logo.

parc

    (A) It stands for Palo Alto Research Center Incorporated.
    (B) It is a research and development company in California.
    (C) It is well known for important development as laser printing, ethernet and GUI.
    (D) All of these

22. Identify the following.
    ■ It is a match-three puzzle video game.
    ■ It was released in 2012.
    ■ Its characters are Tiffi, Mr. Toffee and Easter Bunny.
    (A) Candy Crush Saga
    (B) Angry Birds
    (C) Flow Puzzle
    (D) Flow Loops

23. Mountain Lion, Mavericks and Yosemite are versions of operating system, associated with ___________ computers, developed by Apple Inc.
    (A) Windows
    (B) Macintosh
    (C) Super
    (D) Both (A) and (C)

24. Smart Covers in tablet computers are used to __________.
    (A) Protect the touchscreen and save energy
    (B) Fix the device to a wall
    (C) Type and input text
    (d) Provide internet connectivity

25. __________ is a peer-to-peer file transfer protocol for sharing large amount of data over the internet, in which each part of a file downloaded by a user is transferred to other users.
    (A) Torrent
    (B) BitTorrent
    (C) ClipTorrent
    (D) DownTorrent

─Darken Your Choice with HB Pencil─

1.	Ⓐ Ⓑ Ⓒ Ⓓ	6.	Ⓐ Ⓑ Ⓒ Ⓓ	11.	Ⓐ Ⓑ Ⓒ Ⓓ	16.	Ⓐ Ⓑ Ⓒ Ⓓ	21.	Ⓐ Ⓑ Ⓒ Ⓓ
2.	Ⓐ Ⓑ Ⓒ Ⓓ	7.	Ⓐ Ⓑ Ⓒ Ⓓ	12.	Ⓐ Ⓑ Ⓒ Ⓓ	17.	Ⓐ Ⓑ Ⓒ Ⓓ	22.	Ⓐ Ⓑ Ⓒ Ⓓ
3.	Ⓐ Ⓑ Ⓒ Ⓓ	8.	Ⓐ Ⓑ Ⓒ Ⓓ	13.	Ⓐ Ⓑ Ⓒ Ⓓ	18.	Ⓐ Ⓑ Ⓒ Ⓓ	23.	Ⓐ Ⓑ Ⓒ Ⓓ
4.	Ⓐ Ⓑ Ⓒ Ⓓ	9.	Ⓐ Ⓑ Ⓒ Ⓓ	14.	Ⓐ Ⓑ Ⓒ Ⓓ	19.	Ⓐ Ⓑ Ⓒ Ⓓ	24.	Ⓐ Ⓑ Ⓒ Ⓓ
5.	Ⓐ Ⓑ Ⓒ Ⓓ	10.	Ⓐ Ⓑ Ⓒ Ⓓ	15.	Ⓐ Ⓑ Ⓒ Ⓓ	20.	Ⓐ Ⓑ Ⓒ Ⓓ	25.	Ⓐ Ⓑ Ⓒ Ⓓ

LOGICAL REASONING

LEARNING OBJECTIVES

➤ Tips to solve analogy questions
➤ Concept of Odd one out
➤ Alphabet series concepts
➤ Different types of blood relation
➤ Different directions and their concept
➤ Row seating arrangement
➤ Circle seating arrangement

➤ Concept of statements and their logical conclusion
➤ Concept of embedded figures
➤ Questions on mathematical operations and number puzzles
➤ Different types of Venn diagram
➤ Concept of analytical reasoning questions

MULTIPLE CHOICE QUESTIONS

1. Which one of the following letters is exactly midway between 6th letter and 14th letter in the English alphabet?

   (A) J   (B) H
   (C) G   (D) N

2. If the letters of the English alphabets is written in the reverse order and every alternate letter starting from W, is deleted, which letter will be exactly in the middle?

   (A) M
   (B) O
   (C) N
   (D) M or O

3. If the second half of the English alphabet is written in reverse order which letter will be 6th to the left of the letter which is 10th from the right?

   (A) J   (B) K
   (C) L   (D) M

4. Find the odd one out.

   (A) Cup
   (B) Plate
   (C) Page
   (D) Spoon

5. Find the odd one out.

   (A) Darjeeling
   (B) Gangtok
   (C) Dispur
   (D) Lucknow

6. Find the odd one out.

   4 8 16 32 62

   (A) 4
   (B) 8
   (C) 16
   (D) 62

Directions (7-9): In each of the following letter series, some of the letters are missing, which are given in such order as one of the alternatives below it. Choose the correct alternative.

7. _ op _ mo _ n _ _ pnmop _.
   (A) mnpmon
   (B) mpnmop
   (C) mnompn
   (D) mnpomn

8. _bcc _ ac _ aabb _ ab _ cc
   (A) aabca
   (B) abaca
   (C) bacab
   (D) bcaca

9. m _ nm _ n _ an _ a _ ma _
   (A) aamnan
   (B) ammanm
   (C) aammnn
   (D) amammn

Directions: Each of these questions is based on the following information:

   A + B means A is the mother of B.

   A − B means A is the sister of B.

   A * B means A is the father of B.

   A β B means A is the brother of B.

10. Which of the following means Q is the grandfather of P?
    (A) P + N * M * Q
    (B) Q * N * M + P
    (C) Q β M β N * P
    (D) None of these

11. Which of the following means that N is the maternal uncle of M?
    (A) N β P − L + E − M
    (B) N − Y + A β M
    (C) M − Y * P − N
    (D) N β C + F * M

12. Pointing to a photograph of a boy Sanjay said, "He is the son of the only daughter of my father." How is Sanjay related to that boy?

    (A) Sister
    (B) Uncle
    (C) Cousin
    (D) Father

13. One morning after sunrise, Shraddha and Shubhra were standing in a chowk in Rai Bareily with their back towards each other. Shraddha shadow fell exactly towards her right hand side. Which direction was Shubhra facing?
    (A) East
    (B) West
    (C) North
    (D) South

14. A girl was going towards east. She turns left than turned 90°. A girl was going towards east. She turned left and then turned 90° in anti-clockwise direction. In which direction was she going now?
    (A) East
    (B) West
    (C) North
    (D) South

15. Golu walks 1 km Southwards takes a left turns, walks 6 km, then turns left, walks 5 km and again turning right, walks 5 km. In which direction is he now from the starting point?
    (A) East
    (B) North
    (C) West
    (D) South

Directions (16-18): Five girls are sitting on a bench to be photographed. Shraddha is to the left of Rani and to the right of Tina. Sheetal is to the right of Rani. Reeta is between Rani and Sheetal.

16. Who is sitting immediate right to Reeta?
    (A) Tina
    (B) Rani
    (C) Sheetal
    (D) Shraddha

17. Who is in the middle of the photograph?

   (A) Tina

   (B) Rani

   (C) Reeta

   (D) Shraddha

18. Who is second from the right?

   (A) Sheetal

   (B) Rani

   (C) Reeta

   (D) Tina

Directions (19–21): In each of the following questions two statements are given. Which are followed by four conclusions (1), (2), (3) and (4). Choose the conclusions which logically follow from the given statements.

19. **Statements:** No door is dog. All the dogs are cats.

   Conclusions:

   (1) No door is cat.

   (2) No cat is door.

   (3) Some cats are dogs.

   (4) All the cats are dogs.

   (A) Only (2) and (4)   (B) Only (1) and (3)

   (C) Only (3) and (4)   (D) Only (3)

20. **Statements:** All green are blue. All blue are white.

   Conclusions:

   (1) Some blue are green.

   (2) Some white are green.

   (3) Some green are not white.

   (4) All white are blue.

   (A) Only (1) and (2)

   (B) Only (1) and (3)

   (C) Only (1) and (4)

   (D) Only (2) and (4)

21. **Statements:** All men are vertebrates. Some mammals are vertebrates.

   Conclusions:

   (1) All men are mammals.

   (2) All mammals are men.

   (3) Some vertebrates are mammals.

   (4) All vertebrates are men.

   (A) Only (4)

   (B) Only (2)

   (C) Only (3)

   (D) Only (1)

Directions (22-24): In each of the following questions, you are given a figure (X) followed by four alternative figures (A), (B), (C) and (D) such that figure (X) is embedded in one of them. Find out the alternative figure which contains fig. (X) as its part.

22. Find out the alternative figure which contains figure (X) as its part.

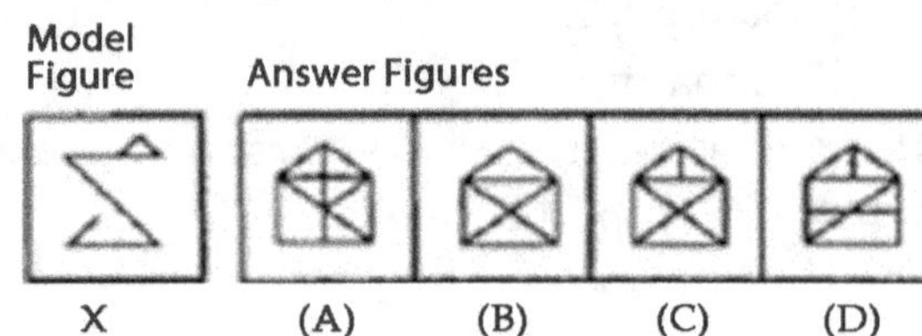

   (A) A

   (B) B

   (C) C

   (D) D

23. Find out the alternative figure which contains figure (X) as its part.

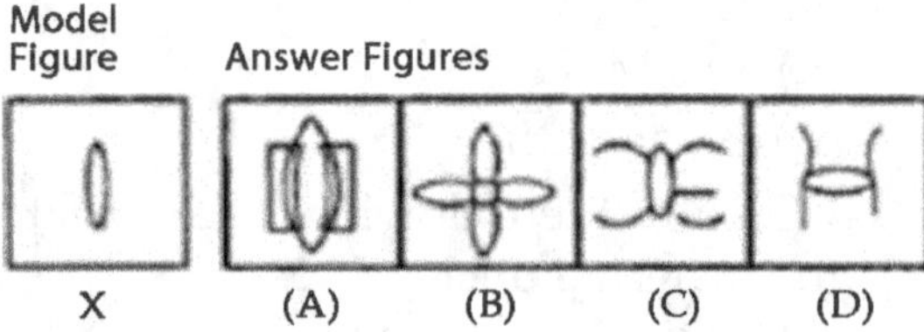

   (A) A

   (B) B

   (C) C

   (D) D

24. Find out the alternative figure which contains figure (X) as its part.

OLYMPIAD WORKBOOK (NCO) CLASS— 7

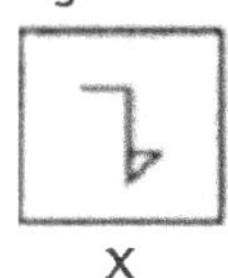 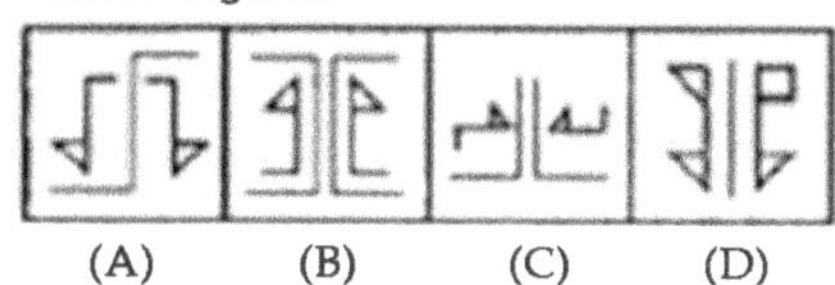

Model Figure — Answer Figures

| X | (A) | (B) | (C) | (D) |

(A) A
(B) B
(C) C
(D) D

Directions (25–27): In this type of questions, a figure or a matrix is given in which some numbers are filled according to a rule. A place is left blank. You have to find out a character (a number or a letter) from the given possible answers which may be filled in the blank space.

25. Which one will replace the question mark?

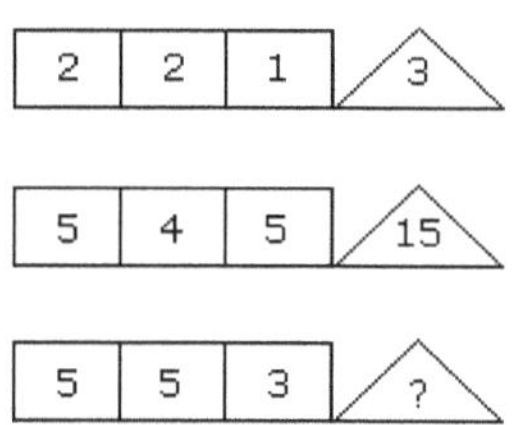

(A) 11
(B) 19
(C) 15
(D) 22

26. Which one will replace the question mark?

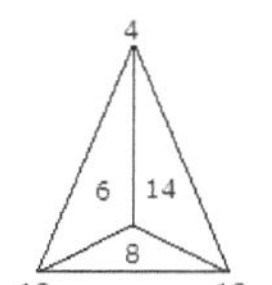 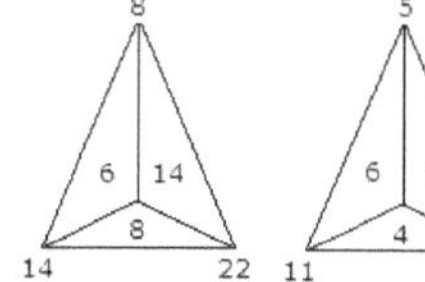

(A) 8   (B) 14
(C) 10   (D) 6

27. Which one will replace the question mark?

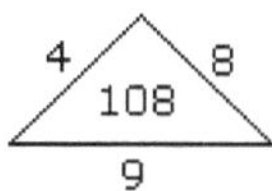 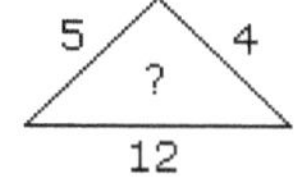

(A) 80
(B) 114
(C) 108
(D) None of these

Directions (28-30): Each of these questions given below contains three elements. These elements may or may not have some inter linkage. Each group of elements may fit into one of these diagrams at (A), (B), (C), (D). You have to indicate the group of elements which correctly fits into the diagrams.

28. Which of the following diagrams indicates the best relation among Author, Lawyer and Singer?

(A) 

(B) 

(C) 

(D) 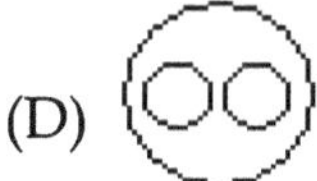

29. Which of the following diagrams indicates the best relation among Factory, Product and Machinery?

(A) 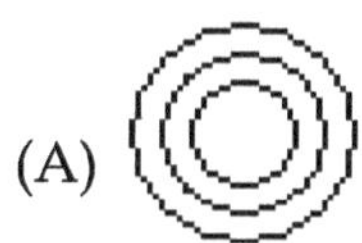

(B) 

(C) 

(D) 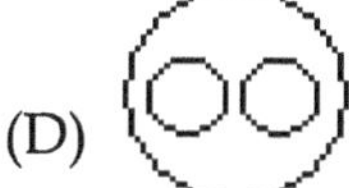

30. Which of the following diagrams indicates the best relation among Women, Mothers and Engineers?

(A)

(B)

(C)

(D)

31. Amit is 15th from the left end of a row of 25 boys and Sumit is 15th from the right end in same row. How many boys are there between them in the same row?
(A) 4   (B) 7
(C) 3   (D) 8

32. If you are 9th in the queue starting either end, how many are there in the queue?
(A) 17   (B) 9
(C) 10   (D) 15

33. Hyderabad is larger than Delhi. Mumbai is larger than Chennai. Bangalore is not as larger as Delhi but larger than Mumbai. Which is the smallest city?
(A) Delhi   (B) Hyderabad
(C) Mumbai   (D) Chennai

34. Rakesh is taller than Hari. Mohit is taller than Rakesh. Dev is taller than Mohit. Surya is the tallest. If they arranged according to their heights, who will be in the middle?
(A) Rakesh   (B) Dev
(C) Hari   (D) Mohit

35. P is older than Q but younger than R. S is younger than T but older than P. If R is younger than S, who is the oldest?
(A) R   (B) T
(C) S   (D) P

MODEL TEST PAPER

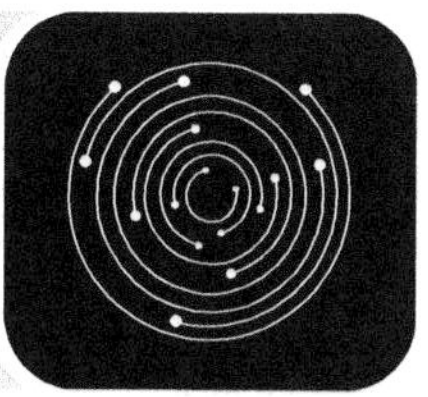

Mental Ability

1. If AE || BF, find the value of x and y respectively.

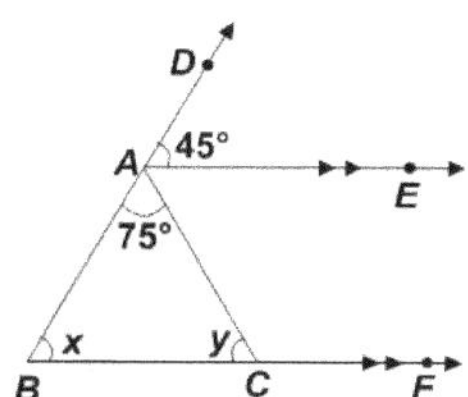

(A) 45°, 65° (B) 60°, 45°
(C) 35°, 75° (D) 45°, 60°

2. Raj bought a glass of mixed juice in which orange, carrot and beet root were present in the ratio 2 : 3 : 1, respectively. If 400 ml of juice accounts for only orange and carrot juices, find the quantity of different juices.

(A) Orange - 160 ml
Carrot - 80 ml
Beet root - 80 ml

(B) Orange - 80 ml
Carrot - 160 ml
Beet root - 240 ml

(C) Orange - 160 ml
Carrot - 240 ml
Beet root - 80 ml

(D) Orange - 240 ml
Carrot - 160 ml
Beet root - 80 ml

3. Five years ago, a father was seven times as old as his daughter. If the present age of the father is 47 years, find the present age of the daughter.
(A) 11 years (B) 6 years
(C) 13 years (D) 40 years

4. According to a survey the number of books read by 20 students during the past three months is as follows:
2, 4, 5, 1, 3, 2, 5, 6, 1, 2, 4, 3, 6, 10, 12, 10, 2, 8, 6, 7
Find the mean of the given data. Also find the number of students who read less than the mean number of books.
(A) 5, 11
(B) 4.95, 10
(C) 3.95, 8
(D) 6.25, 5

5. The temperature at 12 noon was 10°C above zero. If it decreases at the rate of 2°C per hour until midnight, at what time would the temperature be 8°C below zero? What would be the temperature at midnight?
(A) 10 P.M., –10°C (B) 3 P.M., –8°C
(C) 8 P.M., –12°C (D) 9 P.M., –14°C

6. Find the value of x and y respectively in the given figure.

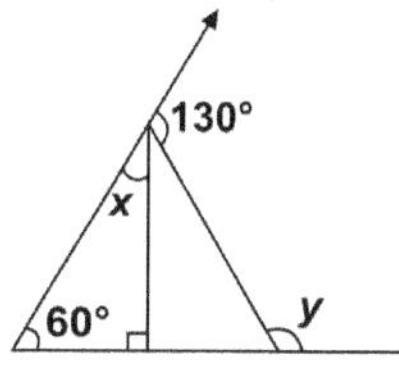

(A) 30°, 150° (B) 20°, 120°
(C) 30°, 110° (D) 60°, 130°

7. Raju sold a TV for ₹8100 suffering a loss of 10%. At what price should he have sold it to gain 10% profit?
(A) ₹9900 (B) ₹9801
(C) ₹9810 (D) ₹9090

8. Find the value of

$$32.78 - 15.43 + \left\{ \frac{855.114}{12.35} - 8.325 \right\}$$

(A) 87.865   (B) 78.265
(C) 63.518   (D) 395.02

9. Rehan got a prize of ₹75,000 in a TV contest. He paid 1/10 of the prize as income tax. Out of the remaining, he gave 1/3 to his son, 1/5 to his daughter, 1/10 to the Red Cross Society and the rest to his wife. How much money did Rehan's wife get?
(A) ₹33,750
(B) ₹67,500
(C) ₹24,750
(D) ₹37,500

10. Rajan borrowed a sum from the bank for 5 years at the rate of 4% p.a. After 5 years, he returned ₹4500. Find the amount borrowed by him.
(A) ₹2735   (B) ₹2505
(C) ₹2475   (D) ₹3750

Logical And Analytical Reasoning

11. Raj is shorter than Mohit. Amit is taller than Raj. Abhishek is taller than Mohit but shorter than Kabir. Mohit is taller than Amit. Who will be in the 4th position if they stand in a row according to their heights in descending order?
(A) Abhishek   (B) Mohit
(C) Amit   (D) Raj

12. If 'INDIA' is coded as 'KLFGC', then how will 'JAPAN' be coded?
(A) KYRYP
(B) HYRYP
(C) LYRYP
(D) LYRYQ

13. Priya walks 1 Km to east and then she turns to South and walks 4 Km. Again she turns to east and walks 2 Km. After this she turns to north and walks 8 Km. How far is she from her starting point?
(A) 4 Km   (B) 5 Km
(C) 8 Km   (D) 10 Km

14. If '+' means '×', '−' means '÷', '×' means '−' and '÷' means '+', then value of 16 ÷ 64 − 8 × 4 + 2 is _______.
(A) 20   (B) 18
(C) 16   (D) 7

15. Pointing to a man in a photograph, Sumit said, "that man's only daughter is my mother". How is Sumit related to that man?
(A) Cousin
(B) Brother
(C) Nephew
(D) Grandson

16. Tanmay remembers that his sister's birthday falls after 7th July but before 12th July while his brother Tarun remembers that his sister's birthday falls after 10th July but before 15th July, on what date does Tanmay's sister birthday fall?
(A) 10th July
(B) 11th July
(C) 12th July
(D) 15th July

17. Which of the following Venn diagrams correctly represents the relation among 'Uncles, Parents, Friends'?

(A)

(B)

(C)

(D)

18. The following question is based on the following set of numbers.
153   364   279   536   298
What is the difference between the middle digits of the highest and the lowest of the above five numbers?
(A) 2   (B) 3   (C) 4   (D) 5

19. Select a figure from amongst the options which will complete Fig. (X).

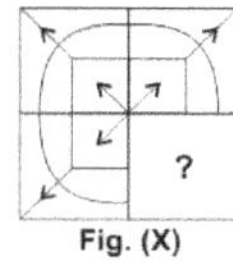

Fig. (X)

(A)   (B)

(C)   (D)

20. How many unit cubes were removed from the solid on the left to obtain the solid on the right?

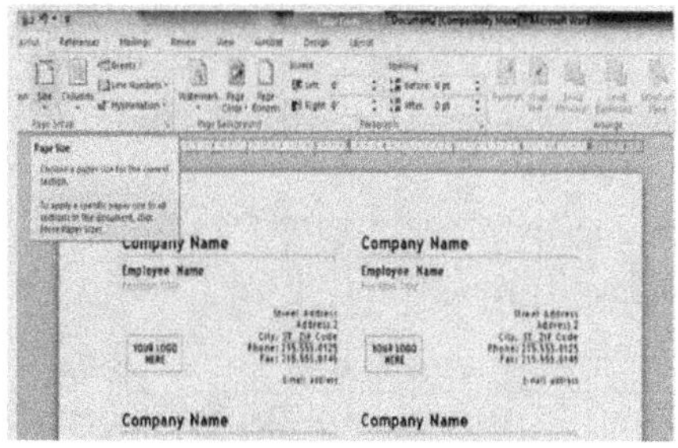

(A) 7   (B) 8   (C) 9   (D) 10

Computers and Information Technology

21. How is the MS Word tab shown in the image below displayed?

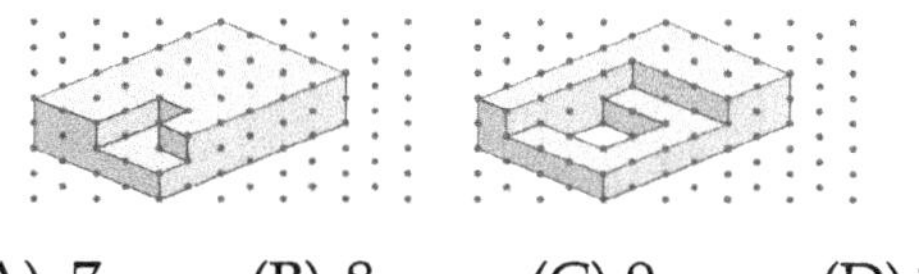

(A) When you create a file from a pre-defined business card template.
(B) When you click on an image, the tools for formatting the image are displayed.
(C) When you create a business card format without using a template.
(D) This is the Home tab of MS Word.

22. Which of the following virus is not a Polymorphic virus?
(A) Melissa
(B) Satan Bug
(C) Tuareg
(D) Elkern

23. The given image is present in _______ tab of MS Excel.

(A) Insert   (B) Home
(C) Data   (D) View

24. Find the odd one out.
(A) Thumb drive
(B) Hard drive
(C) Pen drive
(D) Jump drive

25. This is a format for compressing video with audio at broadcast quality resolution. The output is used for playback in a higher data transfer rate environment. Used usually in the professional market, USB, DVDs and other Video CDs. Identify the most appropriate format.
(A) MPEG-1
(B) MPEG-2
(C) MP3
(D) WAV

26. You have been editing a large MS Word document. Your edits are mainly concentrated around 3-4 locations in the document. Which of the following shortcut keys will quickly take you through all the 3-4 edit points in the document?

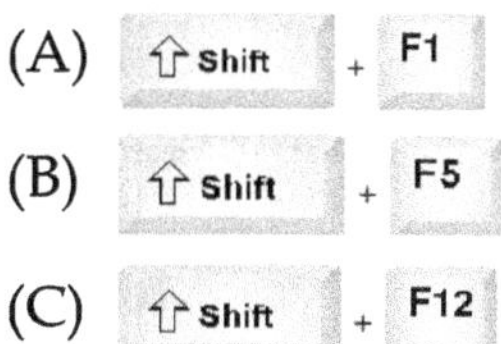

(A) ⇧ Shift + F1

(B) ⇧ Shift + F5

(C) ⇧ Shift + F12

(D) ⇧ Shift + F7

27. _______ is a method to acquire sensitive information like usernames, passwords and banking details – like credit card PINS, etc.
(A) Phishing   (B) Spying
(C) Infecting   (D) Sprucing

28. In image scanners, which of the following device is not used to record how much light is being reflected of an item being scanned?
(A) Cathode Ray Tube
(B) Contact image sensor
(C) Photo multiplier tubes
(D) Charge-coupled devices

29. Which of the following is not a second generation machine?
(A) CDC 1604
(B) PDP-8
(C) Honeywell 400
(D) IBM 7030

30. What will be the output of the following formula in MS Excel?

=SUM(A1:A5, B3:B6)

◢	A	B
1	1	11
2	2	12
3	3	13
4	4	14
5	5	15
6	6	16
7		

(A) 80   (B) 73
(C) 79   (D) 102

31. Match the following.

	Column-I		Column-II
(i)	Organize and store employee information	(a)	Prezi
(ii)	Edit a book or a manuscript	(b)	Safari
(iii)	Play video games with a friend in another country	(c)	Microsoft excel
(iv)	Create budget	(d)	Word Perfect
(v)	Create a tutorial	(e)	Oracle

(A) (i)–(e), (ii)–(d), (iii)–(c), (iv)–(b), (v)–(a)
(B) (i)–(e), (ii)–(d), (iii)–(b), (iv)–(c), (v)–(a)
(C) (i)–(d), (ii)–(e), (iii)–(b), (iv)–(c), (v)–(a)
(D) (i)–(a), (ii)–(e), (iii)–(b), (iv)–(c), (v)–(d)

32. Find the odd one out.

(A)    (B) 

(C)    (D)

33. _____ was the world's first commercially released CD player. It was launched by _____.
(A) CDP-101, Sony
(B) DPC-6800, Panasonic
(C) PT 82, Casio
(D) Zing 89, Yamaha

34. In a computer network, which one of the following network connection devices decides the best path for data transmission from the data source to the destination?
(A) Router
(B) Bridge
(C) Switch
(D) Hub

35. Which of the following computers had a unique feature among other well-known early computers of providing separate processes for handling input/output and processing functions?
(A) EDSAC
(B) UNIVAC
(C) ENIAC
(D) EDVAC

36. _____ scanners are also known as film scanners as they can easily scan the original image of the film.
(A) Handheld   (B) Flatbed
(C) Drum   (D) Slide

37. Which of the following types of processing is used in controlling robots?
(A) Interactive
(B) Real time
(C) Batch
(D) None of these

38. Which of the following is not a mobile communication technology?
(A) GSM (B) EDGE
(C) 3G   (D) VoIP

39. Which of the following is the first Phablet of Acer recently launched in June 2013?
(A) Liquid S1
(B) P3
(C) Liquid mini
(D) Liquid Metal

40. Identify the following.
- A social networking site.
- Founded by Michael and Xochi Birch in January 2005.
- The site was acquired by AOL which turned out to be a worst deal.
(A) Facebook
(B) Twitter
(C) Bebo
(D) Tumblr

41. In MS Word, this button is used to ____.

(A) Insert an image into the document
(B) Apply text wrapping to an image
(C) Crop an image to it the document
(D) Insert a caption to a picture of other image

42. The following icon represents ______ and is found under ________ tab in MS PowerPoint.
(A) Action, Insert
(B) Hyperlink, Insert
(C) Custom animation, Animation
(D) Action, Home

43. In MS PowerPoint, which of the following options is used to share the presentation with remote users who can watch in a web browser?

(A)   (B)

(C)   (D)

44. Which keyboard shortcut allows you to create an embedded chart of the data in the current range in MS excel?
(A) Alt + F1 (B) F11
(C) F12   (D) F1

45. Homegroup option is found under ______ category of Control Panel in Windows 7.
(A) Ease of Access
(B) Network and Internet
(C) System and Security
(D) Appearance and Personalization

Achievers Section

46. What is the output of the given QBASIC code?
```
S = 1
FOR I = 1 TO 15 STEP 2
IF I > 12 THEN EXIT FOR
S = S * I
NEXT I
PRINT I
```
(A) 13 (B) 17
(C) 9   (D) 7

47. Identify the system.
- It was an electromechanical device.
- It used over 3000 electrically actuated switches.
- It could perform addition, subtraction, multiplication, division and table reference on as large as 23 digit numbers.
(A) Electronic Delay Storage Automatic Calculator
(B) Electronic Numerical Integrator and Calculator

(C) Universal Automatic Computer One
(D) Mark I Computer

48. Identify the following.
   - A type of port invented by Apple.
   - It transfers large amount of data at very fast speed.
   - It connects camcorders and video equipments to the computer.
   (A) Ethernet Port
   (B) FireWire port
   (C) VGA port
   (D) PS/2 port

49. When a text is selected and marked as Index entry, MS Word adds a special Xe field that includes the marked main entry and _______ information.
   (A) Hyperlink
   (B) Bookmark
   (C) Cross-reference
   (D) Index

50. A _______ is a small screen (CRT or LCD) in an aircraft surrounded by multiple buttons that can be used to display information to the pilot in numerous configurable ways.
   (A) CFD   (B) MFD
   (C) AFD   (D) TFD

Darken Your Choice with HB Pencil

1.	Ⓐ Ⓑ Ⓒ Ⓓ	11.	Ⓐ Ⓑ Ⓒ Ⓓ	21.	Ⓐ Ⓑ Ⓒ Ⓓ	31.	Ⓐ Ⓑ Ⓒ Ⓓ	41.	Ⓐ Ⓑ Ⓒ Ⓓ
2.	Ⓐ Ⓑ Ⓒ Ⓓ	12.	Ⓐ Ⓑ Ⓒ Ⓓ	22.	Ⓐ Ⓑ Ⓒ Ⓓ	32.	Ⓐ Ⓑ Ⓒ Ⓓ	42.	Ⓐ Ⓑ Ⓒ Ⓓ
3.	Ⓐ Ⓑ Ⓒ Ⓓ	13.	Ⓐ Ⓑ Ⓒ Ⓓ	23.	Ⓐ Ⓑ Ⓒ Ⓓ	33.	Ⓐ Ⓑ Ⓒ Ⓓ	43.	Ⓐ Ⓑ Ⓒ Ⓓ
4.	Ⓐ Ⓑ Ⓒ Ⓓ	14.	Ⓐ Ⓑ Ⓒ Ⓓ	24.	Ⓐ Ⓑ Ⓒ Ⓓ	34.	Ⓐ Ⓑ Ⓒ Ⓓ	44.	Ⓐ Ⓑ Ⓒ Ⓓ
5.	Ⓐ Ⓑ Ⓒ Ⓓ	15.	Ⓐ Ⓑ Ⓒ Ⓓ	25.	Ⓐ Ⓑ Ⓒ Ⓓ	35.	Ⓐ Ⓑ Ⓒ Ⓓ	45.	Ⓐ Ⓑ Ⓒ Ⓓ
6.	Ⓐ Ⓑ Ⓒ Ⓓ	16.	Ⓐ Ⓑ Ⓒ Ⓓ	26.	Ⓐ Ⓑ Ⓒ Ⓓ	36.	Ⓐ Ⓑ Ⓒ Ⓓ	46.	Ⓐ Ⓑ Ⓒ Ⓓ
7.	Ⓐ Ⓑ Ⓒ Ⓓ	17.	Ⓐ Ⓑ Ⓒ Ⓓ	27.	Ⓐ Ⓑ Ⓒ Ⓓ	37.	Ⓐ Ⓑ Ⓒ Ⓓ	47.	Ⓐ Ⓑ Ⓒ Ⓓ
8.	Ⓐ Ⓑ Ⓒ Ⓓ	18.	Ⓐ Ⓑ Ⓒ Ⓓ	28.	Ⓐ Ⓑ Ⓒ Ⓓ	38.	Ⓐ Ⓑ Ⓒ Ⓓ	48.	Ⓐ Ⓑ Ⓒ Ⓓ
9.	Ⓐ Ⓑ Ⓒ Ⓓ	19.	Ⓐ Ⓑ Ⓒ Ⓓ	29.	Ⓐ Ⓑ Ⓒ Ⓓ	39.	Ⓐ Ⓑ Ⓒ Ⓓ	49.	Ⓐ Ⓑ Ⓒ Ⓓ
10.	Ⓐ Ⓑ Ⓒ Ⓓ	20.	Ⓐ Ⓑ Ⓒ Ⓓ	30.	Ⓐ Ⓑ Ⓒ Ⓓ	40.	Ⓐ Ⓑ Ⓒ Ⓓ	50.	Ⓐ Ⓑ Ⓒ Ⓓ

OLYMPIAD WORKBOOK (NCO) CLASS— 7

HINTS AND SOLUTIONS

1. FUNDAMENTALS OF COMPUTER

Answer Key

1. (A)	2. (D)	3. (B)	4. (D)	5. (B)	6. (C)	7. (A)	8. (D)	9. (A)	10. (D)
11. (C)	12. (B)	13. (D)	14. (A)	15. (C)	16. (D)	17. (A)	18. (B)	19. (B)	20. (A)

HOTS (ACHIEVERS SECTION)

21. (A)	22. (B)	23. (A)	24. (B)	25. (B)

2. MEMORY AND STORAGE DEVICES

Answer Key

1. (A)	2. (A)	3. (C)	4. (C)	5. (A)	6. (A)	7. (B)	8. (D)	9. (B)	10. (A)
11. (C)	12. (D)	13. (D)	14. (A)	15. (B)	16. (A)	17. (C)	18. (B)	19. (B)	20. (A)

12. (D)

Option (D) is of RAM (Random Access Memory), which is a primary memory of a computer.

15. (B)

For mass storage, only those devices are used which can retain data for long time and RAM is volatile storage medium which loses its content during power failures.

HOTS (ACHIEVERS SECTION)

21. (C)	22. (A)	23. (C)	24. (A)	25. (B)

22. (A)

SIMM is a memory module (circuit board) that holds the memory chips. The common type of memory module that consists of either 30 or 72 pins.

23. (C)

The BIOS chip initializes hardware components and starts the boot process when a computer is powered on.

24. (A)

Hard drives typically have the highest storage capacity among the options listed.

25. (B)

ROM (Read-Only Memory) is used to store the computer's firmware and BIOS.

3. EVOLUTION OF COMPUTER

Answer Key

1. (B)	2. (B)	3. (C)	4. (D)	5. (C)	6. (C)	7. (B)	8. (D)	9. (D)	10. (A)
11. (D)	12. (B)	13. (D)	14. (B)	15. (A)	16. (B)	17. (B)	18. (C)	19. (B)	20. (D)

HOTS (ACHIEVERS SECTION)

21. (C)	22. (B)	23. (B)	24. (C)	25. (B)

4. WINDOWS 10

Answer Key

1. (C)	2. (B)	3. (C)	4. (A)	5. (D)	6. (B)	7. (A)	8. (A)	9. (C)	10. (A)
11. (B)	12. (A)	13. (D)	14. (C)	15. (C)	16. (E)	17. (E)	18. (B)	19. (D)	20. (C)

HOTS (ACHIEVERS SECTION)

21. (B)	22. (A)	23. (D)	24. (D)	25. (C)

5. MS WORD

Answer Key

1. (B)	2. (A)	3. (C)	4. (A)	5. (B)	6. (C)	7. (B)	8. (B)	9. (D)	10. (A)
11. (D)	12. (C)	13. (A)	14. (D)	15. (B)	16. (B)	17. (A)	18. (C)	19. (A)	20. (B)

HOTS (ACHIEVERS SECTION)

21. (C)	22. (B)	23. (D)	24. (D)	25. (A)

6. MS POWERPOINT

Answer Key

1. (B)	2. (D)	3. (C)	4. (C)	5. (A)	6. (C)	7. (D)	8. (D)	9. (B)	10. (A)
11. (D)	12. (D)	13. (A)	14. (A)	15. (D)	16. (C)	17. (C)	18. (B)	19. (B)	20. (B)

| 21. (B) | 22. (A) | 23. (B) | 24. (A) | 25. (D) |

7. MS EXCEL

Answer Key

| 1. (A) | 2. (C) | 3. (B) | 4. (C) | 5. (C) | 6. (C) | 7. (C) | 8. (D) | 9. (D) | 10. (C) |
| 11. (A) | 12. (B) | 13. (D) | 14. (A) | 15. (A) | 16. (B) | 17. (C) | 18. (C) | 19. (A) | 20. (B) |

HOTS (ACHIEVERS SECTION)

| 21. (B) | 22. (A) | 23. (B) | 24. (A) | 25. (D) |

8. PROGRAMMING IN QBASIC

Answer Key

| 1. (D) | 2. (A) | 3. (A) | 4. (A) | 5. (C) | 6. (A) | 7. (B) | 8. (A) | 9. (D) | 10. (A) |
| 11. (A) | 12. (D) | 13. (A) | 14. (D) | 15. (C) | 16. (D) | 17. (D) | 18. (B) | 19. (D) | 20. (B) |

HOTS (ACHIEVERS SECTION)

| 21. (A) | 22. (B) | 23. (D) | 24. (D) | 25. (A) |

9. INTERNET AND VIRUSES

Answer Key

| 1. (D) | 2. (D) | 3. (D) | 4. (D) | 5. (B) | 6. (B) | 7. (B) | 8. (C) | 9. (C) | 10. (D) |
| 11. (D) | 12. (B) | 13. (D) | 14. (A) | 15. (A) | 16. (A) | 17. (B) | 18. (A) | 19. (C) | 20. (D) |

HOTS (ACHIEVERS SECTION)

| 21. (C) | 22. (D) | 23. (B) | 24. (B) | 25. (B) |

Answer Key

1. (C)	2. (B)	3. (D)	4. (A)	5. (B)	6. (D)	7. (C)	8. (D)	9. (B)	10. (C)
11. (B)	12. (B)	13. (A)	14. (A)	15. (C)	16. (C)	17. (D)	18. (B)	19. (A)	20. (A)

HOTS (ACHIEVERS SECTION)

21. (B)	22. (D)	23. (D)	24. (C)	25. (B)

11. LATEST DEVELOPMENTS IN 'IT'

Answer Key

1. (D)	2. (B)	3. (D)	4. (D)	5. (D)	6. (D)	7. (C)	8. (B)	9. (C)	10. (D)
11. (D)	12. (A)	13. (D)	14. (A)	15. (B)	16. (A)	17. (A)	18. (A)	19. (B)	20. (B)

HOTS (ACHIEVERS SECTION)

21. (D)	22. (A)	23. (B)	24. (A)	25. (B)

12. LOGICAL REASONING

Answer Key

1. (A)	2. (B)	3. (B)	4. (C)	5. (D)	6. (D)	7. (A)	8. (C)	9. (C)	10. (D)
11. (A)	12. (B)	13. (C)	14. (B)	15. (A)	16. (C)	17. (B)	18. (C)	19. (D)	20. (A)
21. (C)	22. (C)	23. (C)	24. (A)	25. (D)	26. (C)	27. (C)	28. (B)	29. (D)	30. (A)
31. (A)	32. (A)	33. (D)	34. (D)	35. (B)					

1. **(A)**
   10th letter comes in between 6th and 14th letter. 10th letter is J.

7. **(A)**
   The series is mopn/mopn/mopn/mopn. Thus, the pattern 'mopn' is repeated.

8. **(C)**
   The series is bbccaa/ccaabb/aabbcc. Thus, the letter pairs move in a cyclic order.

9. **(C)**
   The series is man/man/man/man/man. Thus, the pattern 'man' is repeated.

25. **(D)**
   $(2 \times 2 - 1) = 3$
   and $(5 \times 4 - 5) = 15$
   $(5 \times 5 - 3) = 22$

26. **(C)**
   For first triangle,
   $$10 - 4 = 6$$
   $$18 - 10 = 8$$
   $$18 - 4 = 14$$
   For second triangle,
   $$14 - 8 = 6$$

$$22 - 14 = 8$$
$$22 - 8 = 14$$

For third triangle,
$$11 - 5 = 6$$
$$15 - 11 = 4$$
$$15 - 5 = 10$$

27. (C)

$$(4 + 8) \times 9 = 108$$
$$(5 + 4) \times 12 = 108$$

28. (B)

All the three are different professions.

29. (D)

Product and Machinery are different from each other but both are found in Factory.

30. (A)

All mothers are women and some mothers and some women may be engineers.

MODEL TEST PAPER

Answer Key

1. (D)	2. (C)	3. (A)	4. (B)	5. (D)	6. (C)	7. (A)	8. (B)	9. (C)	10. (D)
11. (C)	12. (C)	13. (B)	14. (C)	15. (D)	16. (B)	17. (A)	18. (A)	19. (A)	20. (D)
21. (A)	22. (A)	23. (B)	24. (B)	25. (D)	26. (B)	27. (A)	28. (A)	29. (B)	30. (B)
31. (B)	32. (D)	33. (A)	34. (A)	35. (B)	36. (D)	37. (B)	38. (B)	39. (A)	40. (C)
41. (D)	42. (A)	43. (A)	44. (A)	45. (B)	46. (A)	47. (D)	48. (D)	49. (C)	50. (B)

SAMPLE OMR ANSWER SHEET

1. STUDENT NAME (IN ENGLISH CAPITAL LETTERS ONLY)

Students must write and darken the respective circles completely using HB Pencil only. Othewise their Answer Sheets will not be evaluated.

PERSONAL DETAILS

2. SCHOOL CODE

3. CLASS

4. SECTION

5. ROLL NO.

6. QUESTION PAPER SET

A ○
B ○
C ○
D ○

7. MOBILE NUMBER

8. GENDER

MALE ○
FEMALE ○

9. STREAM
(Only for Class XI and XII Students)

MATHEMATICS ○
BIOLOGY ○
OTHERS ○

MARK YOUR ANSWERS

No.					No.				
1.	A	B	C	D	26.	A	B	C	D
2.	A	B	C	D	27.	A	B	C	D
3.	A	B	C	D	28.	A	B	C	D
4.	A	B	C	D	29.	A	B	C	D
5.	A	B	C	D	30.	A	B	C	D
6.	A	B	C	D	31.	A	B	C	D
7.	A	B	C	D	32.	A	B	C	D
8.	A	B	C	D	33.	A	B	C	D
9.	A	B	C	D	34.	A	B	C	D
10.	A	B	C	D	35.	A	B	C	D
11.	A	B	C	D	36.	A	B	C	D
12.	A	B	C	D	37.	A	B	C	D
13.	A	B	C	D	38.	A	B	C	D
14.	A	B	C	D	39.	A	B	C	D
15.	A	B	C	D	40.	A	B	C	D
16.	A	B	C	D	41.	A	B	C	D
17.	A	B	C	D	42.	A	B	C	D
18.	A	B	C	D	43.	A	B	C	D
19.	A	B	C	D	44.	A	B	C	D
20.	A	B	C	D	45.	A	B	C	D
21.	A	B	C	D	46.	A	B	C	D
22.	A	B	C	D	47.	A	B	C	D
23.	A	B	C	D	48.	A	B	C	D
24.	A	B	C	D	49.	A	B	C	D
25.	A	B	C	D	50.	A	B	C	D

Signature of the Student & Date of Examination

Signature of the Invigilator & Date of Examination

V&S Publishers, F-2/16 Ansari Road, Daryaganj, New Delhi-110002, ☎ 011-23240026-27
✉ info@vspublishers.com, 🌐 www.vspublishers.com